Simply Victorious for Life

Simply Victorious for Life

30+ Daily Devotionals for Spiritual Enlightenment,
Empowerment, and Illumination
of the Mind, Body, and Soul

JENNIFER WORKMAN

RESOURCE *Publications* • Eugene, Oregon

SIMPLY VICTORIOUS FOR LIFE
30+ Daily Devotionals for Spiritual Enlightenment, Empowerment, and Illumination
of the Mind, Body, and Soul

Resource Publications
An Imprint of Wipf and Stock Publishers
199 W. 8th Ave., Suite 3
Eugene, OR 97401

www.wipfandstock.com

PAPERBACK ISBN: 978-1-5326-5963-8
HARDCOVER ISBN: 978-1-5326-5964-5
EBOOK ISBN: 978-1-5326-5965-2

Manufactured in the U.S.A.   09/27/18

Contents

Lord, What Shall I Do?

"Seek his will in all you do, and he will show you which path to take
(Proverbs 3:6, NLT)."

WHAT SHALL I DO? Have you ever asked yourself that question? Have you ever been in a situation that seemed daunting and overwhelming? If you have answered "Yes" to any of these questions, then you are in good company! All of us have been at a point in our lives whereas, we needed clarity of direction regarding some crucial decisions that we were making. An excellent example of this is Solomon in the word of God i.e. "You made me king . . . but I am like a child . . . Give me an understanding heart so that I can govern your people well and know the difference between right and wrong (I Kings 3:7, 9, NLT)." Even though Solomon was a well-respected and prominent leader, he recognized the sovereignty of God and that only God could lead him down the right path. And, as Solomon, we need to seek God and his direction for our lives for the Bible indisputably states that "for us not to lean to our own understanding but in all our ways acknowledge God and he will direct our paths" (Proverbs 3:6, NKJV).

God is everywhere, God is all knowing and God is the "Alpha and the Omega," the beginning and the end (Revelation 1:8, NKJV)." We can't go wrong when we allow God to spearhead and orchestrate every arena of our lives. Contrastingly, if we become prideful, arrogant and "self-seeking," the final result will be destruction i.e. "There is a way that seems right to a man, but its end is the way of death (Proverbs 14:12, NKJV)." To add, the Apostle Paul was a prisoner on board a ship headed from Palestine to Rome. After they ventured through the Mediterranean Sea and docked at the island of Crete, God told Paul to advise the crew not to leave the harbor because there was going to be a great storm but they didn't listen and they ended up shipwreck (Acts chapter 27).

When asking the Lord, what shall I do? It is imperative to talk to the Lord and not listen to ourselves, the chatter of others or what appear to be the best scenario at the time. For instance, the Bible highlights the fact that "the officer in charge listened more to the ship's captain than to Paul (Acts 27:11, NLT)." When asking the Lord what shall I do? We can't afford to receive wrong counsel because it could be the difference between "life and death" and many times people often give advice from skewed or contaminated lenses based on their personal experiences or things they have encountered in life (Proverbs 28:10, NLT).

Earlier in one of my articles, I used the example in (I Samuel 16:6, NLT) to specify how Samuel used human understanding or finite knowledge to choose God's next appointed king i.e. "when Samuel took one look at Eliab, he thought, "Surely this is the Lord's anointed." And, as a result, God had to remind Samuel "Not to judge based on his appearance or height, for God had rejected him. The Lord continues to express to Samuel the fact that "He doesn't see things the way Samuel sees them and that people judge by outward appearance, but the Lord looks at the heart." In other words, your eyes can steer you in the wrong direction but "listening to God's voice . . . can keep you on track (Proverbs 3:6, TM)."

Yes, God will keep us on track if we ask him too i.e. "one day Elisha and his servant awoke to find their house surrounded by an army of soldiers, as a result, Elisha's servant became hysterical and asked a pertinent question, "what are we going to do?" Elisha then prayed to the Lord to open his servant's eyes so that he may see (II Kings 6:17, NIV)." And, when seeking direction and asking the Lord, what shall I do? We need to pray to God likewise to "open our eyes that we may see wonderful things (Psalm 119:18, NIV)."

I know many times in my own life, when I was faced with difficult decisions to make, I consulted with the Lord. I asked for his will to be performed in my life and to guide me as he saw fit because he is God and he is in control. And, although I didn't have any idea of the final outcome or what God was doing, I had faith that it would all work out for my good "because my father knows exactly what I need (Matthew 6:8, NLT)."

So, in conclusion, anytime you need the question answered Lord, what shall I do? God is open and receptive to hear from you. Don't pick up the phone, don't say what you are going to do and please don't listen to unwise counsel from others. Instead, make connection with God through prayer, meditation and study of his word and through quiet time in his presence.

For in the presence of the Lord, you will receive clear direction and instructions for life, you will receive joy inexpressible and come out with a peace unfathomable, knowing you have made contact with God, that he loves you very much and that he is equipped to appropriately handle your situation.

For You to Ponder: What are you seeking the Lord for? Take time daily to sit in his presence, meditate on his word and let him minister to your heart to receive clear direction and guidance for your life.

I Will Arise

"Do not rejoice over me, my enemy; when I fall, I will arise; when I sit in darkness, the Lord will be a light to me (Micah 7:8, NKJV)."

GETTING BACK UP AFTER a fall is never easy for it requires a great deal of stamina to pull yourself up from a horizontal position to a vertical position. I remember viewing a Track and Field meet on television and watching two seasoned female athletes compete against each other. It was obvious from looking at both of them that they were in superb physical condition and have prepared themselves for this hurdling competition. As they and all the other female competitors took their marks, you could see the determination and focus in both of these women's eyes. Then the gun was shot in the air, they were off and began to run very fast and leap over the hurdles. One by one they jumped and these two ladies were very close in proximity to each other that it would be hard to determine who would win the race, until all of a sudden, out of nowhere, one of the ladies unexpectedly trips and falls over the hurdles. And, it was a hard fall indeed as the audience gasped in shock.

The cameras focused on her as it was evident from her facial expression, that she was very upset and disappointed but then, she composed herself, got up and left off the asphalt as people clapped to show that she gave a great performance and the other lady ended up winning the race. Note, this was not the first time these two ladies competed against each other and the other lady (Dominick) won the race earlier and this was Queen's chance to get the victory this time and when this unforeseen occurrence happened, it was a hard pill for her to swallow! Even though that was the case, she never stopped running nor gave up on her dreams and she continues to run competitively and is preparing herself for the next track meet as she is very tenacious and has etched in her mind that she will win the next race!

Although I am very impressed with Queen's drive and determination to win, I pose the question to you that are reading this article today, isn't that how life is sometimes? We as people seem to do all the right things and give all that we have to move forward just to meet with a fall, unforeseen tragedy or other overwhelming situations just like this female runner. And, that can make us want to give up if we view and respond to our mishaps the wrong way. Life is a journey, it is very difficult at times and sometimes when we think that things are getting easier, they may get worse before they get better but, one thing we as people need to keep in mind is that we are not alone in our struggles "for God promised to never leave us nor forsake us (Hebrews 13:5, NKJV)." He also told us to count it all joy when we fall into diver's temptations (James 1:2, NKJV)."

As we extract the word "temptations" from the previous biblical quote, I ask you what is it you are being tempted by at this moment that would make you not want to get back up after a fall? Surely all of us have fallen in some area of our lives and it would appear that it would be so much easier to stay down but we must get back up! Yes, get back up despite the feeling of apathy, get back up despite the depression, get back up despite the "naysayers," get back up despite the lies the devil is telling you, get back up despite your own negative talk and the things you say to yourself that have hindered you in the past. Whatever you do, just don't stay motionless. Move!

Yes, move! Be like the four men with leprosy indicated in the Bible. They were in a dilemma, they were hungry and they had a skin condition that was contagious but despite all of their problems, they knew that they couldn't remain in the state that they were in i.e. "Why should we sit here waiting to die?" We will starve if we stay here, but with the famine in the city, we will starve if we go back there. So we might as well go out and surrender to the Arameans army. If they let us live, so much the better. But if they kill us, we would have died anyway (II Kings 7:3, 4, NLT)." You have heard the expression "nothing from nothing leaves nothing!" You can't expect anything if you don't do something! I would much rather be found doing something than nothing at all and that was the mentality of the leprous men. So, we can't allow our circumstances to paralyze us and make us fearful. Irrespective of it all, we must move in faith believing as the word of God indicated that "Faith without good deeds is useless (James 2:20, NLT)." We need both in operation in order to produce the desired results.

So tell yourself, I will arise. I will arise because "Greater is he that is in me than he that is in the world (I John 4:4, NKJV)." I will arise because

"Blessed is the man that endureth temptation for when he it tried, he shall receive the crown of life that the Lord has promised to those that love him (James 1:12, NKJV)," I will arise because "Weeping may endureth for a night but joy comes in the morning (Psalms 30:5, NKJV)," I will arise because "Those that sow in tears shall reap in joy (Psalms 126:5, NKJV)" and I will arise because Jesus expressively states "I come that they might have life and that more abundantly (John 10:10, NKJV)."

Nehemiah, although he worked and had people working around him, he needed help from the Lord. We as people need also to recognize our need for God. Yes, we may have money, connections and otherwise but, nothing will happen unless God moves in the mist of things for us. Nehemiah in the mist of all that he encountered asked the Lord to help him. When I think of this I believe what he was asking God to do was empower him to do what he couldn't do within his own strength. When we have God as our guide and spearheading every direction of our lives, I don't care what adversities that we may encounter, what limitations, and what hindrances or otherwise, God will help us to overcome and be victorious in the process.

I don't know about you but I need God to strengthen my hands. I need God to lead me in all things, show me the way, and give me wisdom, understanding and direction in life. I know with his help I am assured victory in the end. I implore you again in all things talk to the Lord in prayer. For in conversation with the Lord, you will receive clear guidance and instruction for life. It is very risky thinking that we as human beings with our "finiteness," knows what is best for ourselves other than the omniscient and infinite God. As you ask him to "strengthen your hands," trust that he knows what is best and is leading you to where he would have for you to go which is far better than what you can fathom as a human being. And, always remember no matter what that "all things work together for good, to them that love the Lord and are called according to his purpose (Romans 8:28, NKJV)."

For You to Ponder: When have you felt like throwing up the surrender flag because of the overwhelming trials and struggles that you have had to encounter? I would challenge you today not to allow your feelings to dictate your responses and press forward in faith believing that if you don't give in, the next step might be your moment of breakthrough.

Lord, Don't Let Time Pass Me By

"For in death there is no remembrance of thee: in the grave who shall give thee thanks (Psalm 6:5, KJV)?"

I WAKE UP DAILY with a renewed sense of purpose and every opportunity that I have, I try to utilize it wisely recognizing life has been given as a gift from the Lord. I am conscience of the fact that God didn't give me this opportunity "unto myself" but to use it as a means to empower and bless others around me. I have heard the expression "life is what you make of it" and although I agree, I also believe that it could be so much more with God spearheading every direction of our lives. The Bible tells us straight-forwardly that to "everything there is a season and a time for every purpose under heaven (Ecclesiastes 3:1, NKJV)". When we go through life with this etched in our minds, it causes us to view and handle life differently.

I have heard Bishop T.D. Jakes make the statement that death doesn't make him afraid but what does cause him great discomfort is living life in regret because he didn't manifest the purpose and plan God orchestrated for his life and therefore, didn't have the opportunity to change things for the better for people and the world around him. I agree wholeheartedly with him and that is why I try to live my life with the mentality of how I can make someone's day and utilize gifts, talents, skills and abilities to the glory of God, so that, when I die, I can rest "at ease" knowing I've fulfilled God's purpose for my life and "didn't let time past me by!"

As I reflect and I am deeply contemplative, I am very thankful to the Lord and praise him for all things and, my continual prayer to the Lord as I start each day is, "Lord, please don't let time past me by." Meaning, don't let time find me in a place whereas I am so focused and enmeshed with the "cares of life," that focusing on those insignificant things keeps me from be-ing effective for the kingdom of God. Don't let time past me by that I don't take time with my family and create memories that are priceless and can't be given back. Please don't let time find me whereas I am so focused on past hurts, failures and disappointments that I allow the "old mentality" to keep me from enjoying every day that have been given as a blessing from God.

Satan has many tactics that he uses to rob us as people from living the best life we can while we are on earth and we shouldn't allow him the space to do so. Again, if we are distracted with "minor issues" that we make "major issues" it keeps us from loving as we should and improving our world as a whole. When people look at us specifically as Christians, they hope to see a difference in our character, behavior and lifestyle. They know what they see daily as "the norm" and if we are no different than the world, then what have the world to look forward to as encouragement or as an example in times of suffering and pain. That isn't to say that we as Christians are "super human" and don't have feelings and are exempt from pain because that is far from the truth but what would be a great sense of encouragement to others in general is to articulate the fact that we all go through and feel pain but to use that "pain" as a tool to bless others.

So, I implore you again, "don't let time pass you by. You have a lot to give and a lot of people to bless in this life. Humbly submit yourselves to God and ask him to help you in the process to be all that he has predestined you to be from the foundations of the earth and "take wings and soar!"

For You to Ponder: Don't give the devil a "foot hole" in your life anymore to rob you of the time that you have been given as a gift from God meditating on things and people that don't add any significance to your life. Instead, invest you time wisely in helping create a better world by helping others and being an asset and not a liabilityandtake time to bless someone today!

Five Steps That Can Turn Your Dreams into Reality

Hold on to Your Dreams and Don't Let Go! Time is fleeting and tomorrow is promised to no one. We don't have time to waste. We must realize the value of life and that it is a gift from God and that we have been placed on this earth to impact others and to bring glory to God. Although that is the case, we must also not devalue our gifts and talents and allow the daily struggles, failures or difficulties to hinder us from pursuing our dreams and moving forward with our lives.

I have seen over the years countless people that have given up on their dreams because with every attempt to progress and accomplish their goals, they have faced many obstacles, barriers and blockages. "No one ever said that anything worth having would be easy." Life is a series of struggles and "quitters never win." It takes tenacity, perseverance and an unshakeable resolve to keep getting up after you have been knocked down several times. Life is like a boxing match:

The two components prepare themselves physically, mentally and emotionally before entering into the ring. They go into the boxing ring with one mindset and that is that there will be "one winner and one loser" and thus, they go in with the expectation they will be the winner. That is how we as people need to be with life and with meeting our goals and aspirations. You can't be so easy to "throw in the towel" because the fight is intense and you sustain a few harsh blows along the way. That is not the time to give up, but that is the time to muster up the strength, position yourself in faith and fight until you come out on the winning side. Here's Five Ways to Stay focused on your dreams:

1. Keep a journal. Whenever you do something to get you a step closer to your goal, jot it down.

2. Stay Positive. Don't allow people, negative thoughts, or otherwise to deter your vision.

3. Pray. Ask God for help, guidance and direction in your life.

4. Stand on the promises of God, you can trust Him when you can't trust anyone else.

5. Hold on and don't let go until your dreams become reality.

For you to Ponder: Go back through the four steps indicated above and incorporate them daily in your life and even write them down and teach them to others to help them stay focused, motivated and on track to reach their specific goals.

Don't Stop You're Almost There

"Don't be weary while doing good, for in due season, you shall reap if you faint not (Galatians 6:9, NKJV),"

HOW MANY TIMES IN life have we missed out on great opportunities and major "turnarounds" in our lives because just at the point of a breakthrough, we gave up and wasn't willing to press forward against the pain, disappointment, hardships, rejection and downfalls that lifecertainly brings! Previously in another article that I've written, I used the analogy of a boxer. The boxer when preparing himself for a match doesn't have a loser mentality but a winner's mentality. Although it may be quite evident that he has a formidable component and that he will eventually withstand some hard blows, pain and otherwise, he believes wholeheartedly that he is going to win.

That is the mentality that we need to adopt in various aspects of our lives. There are many opportunities to succumb to the inevitable trials and tribulations of life. But, it takes a powerful and focused individual to persevere and stay grounded despite it all! Anyone can have a positive attitude and view life optimistically when all is well and they have all that they desire, "that isn't hard at all and is the easy part!" But what has been a great source of inspiration for me, is to hear stories of people like myself who have made mistakes, "missed the mark," and have been "counted out" by others, yet, we still overcome with the victory in Jesus name!

Now, our coming forth with the victory isn't so much about ourselves and our accomplishments, but, it is to minister to and be a blessing to many people we encounter on a daily basis. I'm writing this article to encourage all of you today because I emphasize with you and know what it feels like to want to give up. Especially when you are walking in relationship with God, have messed up, and feel like you can't get up! But the Bible emphatically states, "For we were slaves. Yet our God did not forsake us in our bondage;

11

but he extended mercy to us in the sight of the King of Persia, to revive us, to repair the house of our God, to rebuild its ruins and to give us a measure of revival in our bondage (Ezra 9:8,9, NKJV)."

When I meditate on that particular scripture, it speaks volumes to the unfathomable love of God and his extended mercies towards all of mankind and, it is more than enough reason for us not to give up, but to continue on this journey of life until God's plan and purposes are manifested in our lives for his glory!

Whatever you are facing today, I implore you by the mercies of God to not stop because you are almost there! "Quitters never win." I know that you're tired and have been on this journey for a long time but the word of God expressively states, "Don't be weary while doing good, for in due season, you shall reap if you faint not (Galatians 6:9, NKJV)," also that, "Weeping may endure for a night but joy comes in the morning (Psalms 30:5, NKJV)" and "Write the vision

And make it plain on tablets, that he may run who reads it. For the vision is yet for an appointed time; But at the end it will speak, and it will not lie. Though it tarries, wait for it; because it will surely come, it will not tarry (Habakkuk 2:2-3, NKJV)." Know that God loves you and in the overall scheme of things, everything is working together for your good and most importantly, God will be glorified in this process and throughout your life!

For You to Ponder: Whatever you have been contemplating doing this year but have let it be a dream and not become reality, take this time to set reasonable goals and go for your dreams! Yes, it will be hard but quitters never win! Determine within yourself that every day brings you closer to realizing your dreams but it takes drive, stamina and a "never the less" attitude to keep moving. I don't know what anyone else has told you but I believe in you, so as the Nike slogan says, "Just do it!"

I Desire to Hear Him Say "Well Done"

"His lord said unto him, well done, good and faithful servant; you have been faithful over a few things, I will make you ruler over many things: enter into the joy of your lord Matthew 25:23 (KJB)."

WHAT IS YOUR DESIRE in life? I know the world has told you that your value and significance is interconnected with tangible and worldly things but I would venture to say that life consists of things far greater than what we visibly see and are normally acquainted with! I remember being a young child and being asked by many family members what I wanted to do with my life and even at such a young age, I had a very clear agenda and focus.

My desire have always been to serve God and live for him, not to say that I've always done things the way that God intended, but, that has definitely been my goal, as well as, advancing in my educational pursuits, getting married, having children and having a successful career in the television arena.

Although that is the case, I recognize that I have been given life by God and the wonderful gift of the Holy Spirit not to sit and be idle but to use every spiritual gift that he has given me to glorify his name and tell as many people as possible about him!

So, my question to you today, do you have a relationship with the father? If not, God's arm is extended and open, ready and willing to receive you home! There is nothing that you have done that can stop him from loving you, being concerned about you and your eternal destination. People will tell you to "live your life out loud," and don't be fixated on changing anything, you are fine just the way you are!" My response to that is if we are okay, then there would be no need for God to have sent his son to die on the cross for "perfect people." The Bibles emphatically tells us that "for God so loved the world that he gave his only begotten son, that whoever believeth in him would not perish but have eternal life (John 3:16, NKJV)." We are sinners in need of a savior and thankfully God sent his son Jesus to atone for our sins!

When we came into the world we came in as sinners. In Genesis after the fall of Adam and Eve, we were predisposed to sin and the world as we know it was never the same after that! But, "just as through the disobedience of the one man the many were made sinners, so also through the obedience of the one man the many will be made righteous (Romans 5:19, NIV)." "There is no need to make excuses anymore and "play rush and roulette with your life." God is soon to return and he's is coming for a prepared people. Will you let him into your hearts today? I know the devil is telling you that it isn't necessary "but it is!" Hell and heaven is for real and both have been specifically designed for the just and unjust, for those that have given their lives to the Lord and for those who have rejected him.

If you are like me and you want to be able to hear him say well done, here are a few things that I pray that you will do to surrender your life to Christ:

- First admit that you are sinner and ask the Lord to come into your life, transform you and give you are heart like his. The word of God clearly states that if "you that if you confess with your mouth the Lord Jesus and believe in your heart that God has raised Him from the dead, you will be saved (Romans 10:9, NKJV)."

- Relinquish your own ways and habits, turn from them and turn to God! "Repent of your sins for the Kingdom of Heaven is near (Matthew 3:2, NLT)."

- Draw closer to God every day through study, meditation and daily application of his word in your life (I Timothy 2:15, KJV, Joshua 1:8, NLT).

- "Pray fervently and without ceasing" (I Thessalonians 5:17, NASB) (James 5:16, KJB).

- Daily and consistent spiritual walk with the father through obedience, faithful service and a surrendered life to him, otherwise, we are only "hearers and not doers of the word" (James 1:22, KJV) (John 14:15, KJB) (I Samuel 15:22, NIV) and (Luke 6:46, NIV).

And, remember, just as it took you a while to "dig yourself into the destructive aspects of sin and entangle yourself in the ideas, philosophies and ideologies in this world," so is it going to take that same amount of effort if not more to remain in the alignment and will of the father. A spiritual walk with God "isn't a fly by night thing." It takes having a "made up mind" and being totally surrendered to God and his direction for your life. It is not works based but it is through the power of the Holy Spirit that enables us to live according to God's design for our lives and it is the Holy Spirit that keeps us from day to day! So, my prayer is that someone that have ready this article today will make up their minds to seek after the Lord with all their hearts and surrender all to him because when he returns "my desire is to hear him say "well done," and I hope that will be yours too!"

For You to Ponder: Jesus is coming soon, will you be ready? If there is any doubt in your mind about your eternal destination or you don't have a relationship with God, he is waiting for you. Pray to the Lord and ask him into your life today, don't wait for tomorrow isn't promised to anyone. If you do have a relationship with God, take time to share your faith it others i.e. co-workers, friends and family that don't know God they need him in their lives as well!

Anxiety a Weight too Heavy to Carry

"Why are you cast down, O my soul? And why are you disquieted within me (Psalm 42:5, NKJV)."

DOES THAT SOUND FAMILIAR? If you've answered yes to this question, then you are definitely not alone because that has been the heartfelt cry of many people. A cry for help and relieve amidst the constant weights and pressures of life. Life is very difficult. We as human beings are inundated with various stressors on a daily basis from unexpected family issues, to unending financial strains, to marital issues, etc.

The pressures of trying to live up to a false picture of what the world views as "perfect" and one that is able to be "all things to all people" is a daunting feat indeed! We are in a constant state of arousal and it is "no wonder" why we deal with such a high level of anxiety. The body wasn't created to be under a continual "adrenaline high." You do a lot of "undoable" damage to your body because it isn't equipped to "function effectively when it remains in a perpetual state of tension and arousal ("Christian Counseling-A Comprehensive Guide" By Gary Collins- Pg. 78)." One of the manifestations of being under a constant state of arousal is Depression. The Bible tells us that "anxiety in the heart of a man causes depression (Proverbs 12:25, NKJV)." Also, there are many other mental, physical and emotional affects that anxiety causes on our overall well-being from heart disease, to panic attacks, to aches and pains, to headaches, to anger and "the list goes on and on."

According to the Bible, there is nothing wrong with honestly facing and trying to deal with our problems of life. But it is wrong and unhealthy to be immobilized by excessive worry (Christian Counseling-A Comprehensive

Guide by Gary Collins, pg. 79)." Having this in mind, we really need the help of the Lord to effectively and adequately deal with anxiety. As David states, "Search me, O God, know my heart; try me, and know my anxieties (Psalm 139:23)." Whatever plagues us and is at the center of an "anxious heart," needs to be brought to God in prayer, and it is through prayer, that we connect with God and receive help from God to be able to successfully maneuver the complexities of life.

God is the source of all comfort and is "present" to ease our anxious hearts (Psalm 46:1, NKJV) and (Psalm 94:19, NKJV). "He cares about us and he doesn't want us to carry loads that are impossible for us to carry but release those burdens on his strong and capable shoulders (I Peter 5:7) and (Hebrews 12:1, NKJV)." For God promises to always be with us through our trials and tribulations (Hebrews 13:5, NKJV)." Thank God for his unwavering and indescribable love towards all of mankind!

An unwavering love so strong that he sent his only begotten son Jesus to atone for the sins of all people (John 3:16, NKJV). "Having exemplified that, do you think that God would leave you in the predicament you're in, to crumble under all the negativity and problems of life?" My answer to you is "no!" God loves you unconditionally and if we as people are able to receive his love without limitations, then, we know unequivocally that we can turn over all our cares and concerns of life to him because he is our Father and our "refuge" (Psalm 46:1). "When you can't count on no one or nothing else you can count on God!"

I implore you today to relinquish whatever control you may have over your situation and place it in the powerful hands of God almighty. We spear ourselves from sickness, death and unnecessary pain, when we recognize "who can really handle our problems" and it definitely isn't us but God! I know that this isn't something that some of you can do instantaneously but honestly, "is anything else working? The Bible tells us emphatically for us to cast all our cares upon Him for he cares for us (I Peter 5:7)." Try God because in the long run, what you have to loose other than "weight" that you were not meant to carry!"

For You to Ponder: Relinquish your desire to feel like you are in control of your life. Recognize that God is sovereign and he is in control of your life and the path that you take. You are not "an island to yourself." Pray today and seek the Lord about every direction for your life in terms of family, career, health or whatever the case maybe because he will direct your steps.

Amassing the Kingdom not the Pockets

> What shall I render to the Lord for all of his benefits towards me? I
> will take up the cup of salvation, and call upon the name of the Lord. I
> will pay my vows to the Lord, Now in the presence of all of His people
> (Psalm 116:12, NKJV)."

I BESEECH YOU BRETHREN by the mercies of God that you present your
bodies a living sacrifice, holy acceptable unto God which is your reasonable
service (Romans 12:1, NKJV)."

"Bless the Lord all my soul and all that is within me bless His holy
name." Thank God for yet another privilege to speak as the "Holy Spirit
gives thee utterance." God is an awesome God and worthy of all of the
praises and I am thankful and humbled that he chose me as an instrument
for his glory, that is why I thought it necessary to talk today in reference to
what is our true motivation for what it is that we do as it relates to God's
work and advancing the kingdom? Because like it or not, as Christians our
first focus should be faithful obedience and total submission to God's will
for our lives and serving him until he returns.

It is quite evident as we look all around us that people need God at the
forefront of their lives. They chase after money, status, position, titles and
all the things that the world tells them makes a person whole and complete
but often times more than not, they find that after acquiring these things,
they are still empty and unfulfilled. Why? Because what they are searching
for through things is a fallacy. It isn't things that makes us who we are but it
is God that completes us! So having stated such, we as people of God need
to understand that going after stuff should not be our main focus and objective either but chasing after God and winning souls for him. Too many

people engage or entangle themselves in the cares of life to the neglect of their relationship with God and the Bible tells us emphatically that, that is a tool of the enemy to get us distracted that we may become fruitless (Luke 8:14, NKJV)."

I don't know about you but I desire to live a life that is obedient and surrendered to the will of God. I am not imperfect nor am I claiming to be but it is my desire to serve God while I have time. I recognize that there are innumerable opportunities all around me to bless others and if I allow myself to make money and the "world's goods" my focus then I can't be all God requires me to be. If what I do is motivated by fine cars, fine houses, "people praises," titles, positions and all other insignificant things, then when those things are taken away, my passion and focus goes with it. But if what I am doing is for God's glory and not my own, then no matter what happens on this "side of life," I will keep my eyes upon him, "looking unto God which is the author and finisher of my faith (Hebrews 12:2, KJV)."

I don't know who is reading this article today but I implore you "do all to the glory of God (Colossians 3:17, NKJV)." Let all that you do in life be motivated by your love for God and pleasing him, let all that you do be to see other's lives spiritually transformed and walking in relationship with God. Let all you do not be motivated by money as it is sure " we brought nothing with us when we came into this world, and we can't take anything with us when we leave it (I Timothy 6:7, NLT)," so, let all you do be a testimony of the awesomeness and faithfulness of God in operation in your life so that people may see you more than just another "motivational speaker" or "life coach" but one that is loving, faithful and surrendered to God, living a life that is pleasing in his sight and therefore being "salt and light" unto the earth (Matthew 5:13-16, NKJV)."

God already knows that in order for us to survive on this earth that we need to be able to financially support our families. He knows how the world operates and he knows even the things that you need at this moment but the word of God states that "if you seek first the kingdom of God and all of his righteousness then God in his time will provide the things that you need (Matthew 6:33, NKJV)." If God provided "manna" to the children of Israel (Exodus 16:35, NLT), then surely he knows how to provide for your needs and the needs of your family.

But, it is when we make "mammon" our focus that we fall into many destructive behaviors and are consumed for the Bibles states that "the love of money is the root of all kinds of evil. And some people, craving money, have wandered from the true faith and pierced themselves with many sorrows (I Timothy 6:10, NLT)." And sadly, that same mindset and mentality has also crept into many churches today whereas, the primary motivation for what many ministers, evangelists and others in ministry do is geared toward money. But the Bible is very clear that there is nothing "new under the sun (Ecclesiastes 1:9, NKJV)." And, that there were false prophets in Israel just as there will be false teachers among you. In their greed they will make up clever lies to get hold of your money. But God condemned them long ago, and their destruction will not be delayed (II Peter 2: 1, 3, NLT)."

Yes, "money answers all problems (Ecclesiastes 10:19, KJV)," but if it is used deceptively and as a means to twist and distort the word of God for worldly gain, there are consequences for this sinful and corrupt behavior i.e. "It would be better if they had never known the way to righteousness than to know it and then reject the command they were given to live a holy life (II Peter 2:21, NLT)" and, "Dear friends, if we deliberately continue sinning after we have received knowledge of the truth, there is no longer any sacrifice that will cover these sins (Hebrews 10:26, NLT)." In order words, there is no excuse, when we know better we do better!

In conclusion, hear the truth of the matter, serve God, trust him, let him lead and direct your life and in all that you do, do it in sincerity and with love towards God and love for people in that you tell them the truth of God's word and acquaint them with who God is that they may have life and that more abundantly that is found only in Jesus Christ (John 14:6, NKJV)."

For You to Ponder: Let everything that you do in life be God-centered. Start every day with seeking to know God's will and what he would have for you to do? If you have a financial need, pray to the Lord about providing what you need but don't do anything motivated by money but let all that you do be motivated by your love for others and motivated by your love for God.

Be a true "Good Samaritan" and "Take Action"

> "But a Samaritan, as he traveled, came where the man was; and when he saw him, he took pity on him. He went to him and bandaged his wounds, pouring on oil and wine. Then he put the man on his own donkey, brought him to an inn and took care of him (Luke 10:33-34, NIV)."

PRAISE GOD FOR HIS indescribable love and another opportunity to operate as an instrument for his glory and to enrich hearts, empower minds and above all pray that the article will expose the true motives of the heart, uproot anything that is not like God and consequently bring about spiritual transformation in the lives of every reader.

Who is a "Good Samaritan?" The Bible states indisputably that a Good Samaritan is a "person that goes beyond their comfort zone, engages themselves in the "dirtiness" of other's lives and is willing to aid them in their extreme time of privation (Luke 10:33-35, NIV)" or as Minister Stefan Edgecombe so passionately pontificates on his Facebook post, a "true friend is willing to enter into to your experience." Although the "Good Samaritan" exemplified in this particular scripture is to be commended for his "self-sacrifice" for the benefit of another, I wonder how many people are willing to venture as far as he did for the well-being and advantage of another?

As we look at our world as a whole, there are unlimited opportunities to come alongside and aid people that are in need. For instance, there are many people dealing with unemployment that need help financially, there are many people that are sick and need prayer for healing, there are many people that are "poor" as it relates to not being in relationship with God and need the Gospel of Jesus Christ shared to them so that they have an opportunity to receive salvation and the list "goes on and on." I know that it is hard work engaging yourself in the lives of others. I know you may be faced with some uncomfortable situations that you may not be accustomed to and I know that you "maybe" even "put in harm's way," although the work of helping other's is never an easy task, we must do something because if we don't, we are going to be judged by our heavenly father i.e. "Then the righteous will answer him, saying, 'Lord, when did we see you hungry and feed you, or thirsty and give you drink? And when did we see you a stranger and welcome you, or naked and clothe you? "And when did we see you sick or in prison and visit you?' And the King will answer them, 'Truly, I say to you, as you did it to one of the least of these my brothers, you did it to me (Matthew 25:37-40, ESV).'

People think that they have to travel to another country and feed the poor to be doing something great or noteworthy but something as simple as coming to the aid of a neighbor where you live, going by the homeless shelter and helping to feed the poor or placing money in the hands of a sister that you know is struggling and needs help to buy grocery for her children, all of these are ways to exemplify that of a "Good Samaritan." "Keep in mind," while doing this, your whole motivation is helping others, not fanfare, not a pat on the shoulder but simply coming to the aid of another because when you do this, you will receive your reward from God (Matthew 6:2-4, HCSB)."

Without disclosing too much information because again it is not for "man's glory" but for the glory of God. I remember working on a project for television and the assignment called for me to work in a club setting. The director that I worked with at the time knew that I was a Christian and he respected me as a whole and my beliefs. I worked with many people in the entertainment arena and oftentimes during the taping the music was very loud, the smell of cigarettes and alcohol permeated air and I could have easily succumbed to my "discomfort," if that was my mentality but I went into that setting with the mindset of "how this could be an opportunity to share the Gospel of Jesus Christ to those around me" and the Lord afforded me the opportunity with the young man that I was actually Co-Hosting the show with. God is awesome and the orchestrator of all things and if I would have allowed my personal feelings and being in an "unfamiliar territory" to hinder me from being a "Good Samaritan," then it would have been no bodies fault but my own!

In conclusion, I implore you to always make yourself available to be used by God and to exemplify the "Good Samaritan" in different aspects of your life. You never know that someone could be at a point of giving up on life and/or contemplating suicide and a single gesture in terms of praying for them, encouraging them, reaching into your pockets to help meet a tangible need or just being a listening ear, could make a tremendous difference in their lives because you chose to look beyond yourself and focus on the needs of others. That is the epitome of Jesus's ministry while he was on earth and what we should do in our lives to adequately represent him. "I must work the works of him that sent me, while it is day: the night cometh, when no man can work (John 9:4, KJB)."

For you to Ponder: In what ways can you extend love and help to someone today? I would challenge you to go beyond mere contemplation and seek out ways to help a neighbor, friend, co-worker, homeless person, single mother or someone else in need because when you meet a "tangible or physical need" it makes people more receptive to receive the spiritual food from the word of God.

Before I Say, "I DO"

"He who finds a wife finds a good thing, and obtains favor from the
Lord (Proverbs 18:22, NKJV)."

PEOPLE NOWADAYS ENTER INTO marriage with a very "fantasy-like" ideology of what they believe marriage to be. The bride before the marriage
incorporates countless time facilitating all the different aspects of the wedding ceremony. She wants everything to be perfect. The mother and father
invests a lot of time, money and energy to give their daughter the wedding
of her dreams. The groom is also very excited and anticipatory of seeing his
new bride. But, do either one of them really utilize the time "before I say, I
do" to make sure they are ready and in the place spiritually, psychologically,
emotionally or otherwise to have a successful marriage? Because "like it or
not," there is life beyond the wedding festivities.

Yes, life, that is beyond fancy dresses, tuxedos, intricate bridal designs,
happy faces, great music and luxurious vacations. In reality, that's the easy
part! On the other hand, what is really going to test the couples love, commitment and faithfulness to each other is within the covenant of marriage
itself! That is why before the couple says "I do," they must wholeheartedly
seek the Lord in prayer and ask for wisdom, discernment and direction as
it relates to their relationship in its totality. They need to ask God to open
their spiritual vision and help them to see beyond their natural desires and
inclinations. Why? Because their future mate can have the appearance of
being either "Mr. or Mrs. right," say all the right things and "makes the cut"
on the "mate list," but only God knows the heart, can go beyond the surface
and see the true motives of a person's heart, whether it is pure or not!

To add, before standing before God and our loved ones making a "vow
to love, to cherish" and be faithfully committed to each other, we need to
make sure our mind, body and spirit are deeply interconnected with God.

Our relationship with God is very imperative and will affect all areas of our life. A couple cannot expect to have a strong, productive or healthy relationship if God is not spearheading every part of their lives. They must always recognize God's sovereignty and that "he knows what is best" and they must let God transform their lives and make them more like himself so that they can be fruitful in their marriage. Because there is nothing more powerful and effective in marriage than two people that are spiritually aligned with God!

God is the only one that can allow couples to be Godly mates and loving towards each other. If there is any "emotional baggage" or other issues that want to plague couple's relationships, it is through the power of the Holy Spirit that heals, restores and cleanses them and enable them to be free and not allow old issues to take precedence in their lives nor hinder the stability and productiveness of their marriages. God is also needed at the forefront to help both couples make wise decisions no matter what position they find themselves in life and to be faithful and supportive of each other throughout the good times as well as the bad. Because it is easy to say "I love you" when your spouse is physically healthy and attractive, has a successful career, you both see "eye to eye" and everything seems lovely! But, it takes God's spirit that resides in you, to allow you to stand firm in your relationship with Him as well as your mate when it appears that "all hell is breaking loose" around you and nothing seems to be going right!

So, I implore you again that in all you do, especially as it relates to marriage "make first things first" and seek God's guidance before entering into marriage because it will be the best investment of your time! Let God direct your steps and help you with your "individual self," so that you can bring your "best self" to the marriage. I believe fully with God's help and input, you will be able to move forward and enter into marriage with full assurance knowing that you have God orchestrating your every step and in doing so enabling you to say on your wedding day with full confidence "I do!"

For you to Ponder: A relationship is hard work and nothing to be taken likely. It requires a lot of investment on a person's part to engage another person. A marriage ceremony is just one day but a commitment is a lifetime. So, take time to invest in each other. You may not always agree, you may "fall short" in your actions as human being but God has created you to be relational and all of us need each other.

I'm Homeless, Do You See Me?

Where do I begin? I will begin this article with the fact that homelessness as we know it is epidemic. No where can you go and not visibly see the homeless amongst you for the Bible expressively states that "the poor you will have with you always (Matthew 26:11, NIV)." Although that is quite evident, I wonder do many of us ever stop and think that no matter where these people maybe currently in their lives, they are still very precious and valuable and "have been made in the similitude of God" (Genesis 1:27, NKJV).

Yes God, a God that is so loving and so kind that he looks beyond "outer appearance" and looks at the heart of every individual (I Samuel 16:7, NIV). That is why he loves homeless people as any other people. Why? Because God is more concerned with the condition of our hearts rather than our outer extremities and that is why he sent his son to die on the cross for all of mankind (John 3:16, NKJV).

So, what is it that you see when you see homeless people? Homeless people are not always what society tries to compartmentalize them to be and I would venture to say, you could have someone in close proximity to you in your neighborhood, church, company or otherwise and many out even know that they are homeless. Homeless is the young woman who, although she has tried numerous times to find a job, she's come out empty-handed and as a result, she lost her home and wasn't able to maintain the bills. Homeless is the man who has had a mental issue for a long time and was receiving care from a local mental institution and when the institution was closed, it left him without the psychological and medical care need for stability of his mental faculties and a place to stay. Homeless is the veteran that has served is country faithful for a plethora of years and was severally injured serving his country and then returns home and not be able to get the necessary veterans assistance that he needs, which causes him to become homeless and I can speak to various other scenarios of homelessness but time wouldn't allow.

I used these difference examples to make a point and that point is, things are not always what they appear to be and you can't always judge a book by its cover. Many people here of the stories of successful people like Steve Harvey and Tyler Perry and how they themselves were homeless at one time and it almost seems unbelievable but it is, they were homeless! And like them, many people are battling with homelessness as I speak! To add, I just want to emphasize that I too have been homeless and I know what it feels like and I can sympathize with the plight of the homeless people.

Life isn't easy and we can experience difficulties that shakes us to the core but irrespective of it, God is in control. In conclusion I want to say that God knows where we are, God knows our condition but God has never let our side for he promises emphatically in his word that "he will never leave us nor forsake us" (Hebrews 13:5, NKJV). The Bible also tells not to "lay up for ourselves treasures on the earth, where moth and rust consume, and where thieves break through and steal; but lay up for ourselves treasures in heaven, where neither moth nor (Matthew 16:9, NKJV)." Circumstances change, people change but God never change! I want to encourage someone today that you are not alone in your struggle. There are many people all around this world that feels the way that you do, have the unanswered questions that you have and my response to them and to you is to bring it all to Jesus. For God is the only one that knows how to effectively hand your situation for "God is our refuge and strength, a very present help in trouble (Psalms 46:1, NKJV)." So, If you want to know homeless person if God sees you, if you want to know drug dealer if God sees you, if you want to know single mother if God sees you, he does, for the Bible states that "he never slumbers nor sleeps" (Psalms 121:4, NIV). God cares and if you seek him for the direction of your life and humble ourselves before him, he will give you "abundant life" (John 10:10, NKJV).

Blessings to all of you out there in the struggle of life, you will break through in Jesus name!

For You to Ponder: Stop judging people based on outward appearance! Regardless of people's plight in life, God has created them in his image and they deserved to be loved and respected as any other person. So, extend a hand to offer a word of encouragement, help meet a tangible need or even pray for homeless people or others in need as God gives opportunity because you never know, you maybe where they are at some point in your life!

Don't Hurt Me, Please Help Me!

"A man hath joy by the answer of his mouth: and a word spoken in due season, how good is it (Proverbs15:23, KJV)"

IT HAS ALWAYS BEEN articulated "be careful what you say." Why? Because words are powerful and in them have the ability to "calm the savage beast," and/or create an "atomic bomb" effect in relationships between people. I remember as a child hearing many children sing the song that "sticks and stones may break my bones but words will never hurt me." That song may have been popular for all of us to sing as children growing up but, on the other hand, nothing indicated in the lyrics rings true! Words do hurt and they can affect even the "best of us."

For example, if you have a child that has been raised by very support-ive and loving parents, that constantly articulate and show love towards that particular child, that child is more likely than not to grow up healthy and with a positive outlook on life and themselves. Why? Because of the over-showering of love, support and positive communication from both parents. But, on the other hand, if you have another child that is constantly inundated with negative jargon, unsupportive and unloving parents, they are more than likely to become rebellious and "act out." Why? Because they have been given negative feedback about who they are and thus they inter-nalize this to be true!

That is why it is imperative that we "speak life and not death (Proverbs 18:21, NKJV)" over our children, our loved ones, as well as others. Many marriages and other relationships have been destroyed over harsh and negative words spoken by either person in the "heat of the moment." People have said things to each other that have brutally wounded each other and many still feel the effects of it today! The Bible tells us empathically that "A harsh word stirs up anger but a soft answer turns away wrath (Proverbs

15:1, NKJV)." We can all take a lesson from scripture regarding how we should adequately handle each word that proceeds from our mouths. We are more effective in our communication with each other when we take time to prepare, pray and ask God for wisdom to say the right things, to response in love and to not be so quick to speak but open to hear, for the Bible tells us "Wherefore my beloved brethren, let every man be swift to hear, slow to speak, slow to wrath (James 1:19, KJV)."

We as people deal with enough problems and difficulties every day to last a lifetime. If anything, we embrace positive feedback when we receive it from others. Take for instance, if a person has just lost their loved one, it helps tremendously to have people all around them that exemplifies love and concern for that individual. It also helps to speak soothing and sympathetic words to that person. What helps even more is to have someone that have been where they are and is offering words of comfort and support in a time when they need it most!"

Don't ever underestimate the power of spoken words. Again, they have the power to heal or to wound. I would much rather be on the side of the "healing aspect" of words rather than the "negative effects" of words. My prayer is that God will help all of us to be more wise, discerning and careful in our usage of words and how we relate to each other. Even as we ministry and witness to people all around the world, may we seek the Lord and ask for the power of the Holy Spirit to take over our hearts and minds, and thus equip us to be more effective in our communication of the Gospel of Jesus Christ, as well as, our regular interactions with each other every day, so that when it is all "said and done," may we be at peace in knowing that "we have not hurt but helped others through our words!

For You to Ponder: Words are powerful so make sure that you use them wisely.

Family a True Blessing from the Lord

It is truly a blessing to be connected with family for family is a wonderful blessing from the Lord (Genesis 12:3, NLT).

IN THE FAMILY STRUCTURE we learn much about our rich ancestral history. From out physical appearance, to our proclivities, to our entire biological makeup, it is all interconnected to our family system. Nothing gives us a more succinct picture of who we are than where we come from. For example, when a man chooses a woman as a wife, he oftentimes desires to know more information about the woman's family, why? Because she is a byproduct of her environment.

Regardless of whether we think so or not, family is important and a blessing from the Lord. We are not to devalue each other and the significant parts we play in each other's lives. Just as the body needs each part in order to adequately function, so do we need each other within our families (I Corinthians 12, NKJV). All of us are extremely necessary! Just as Mom and Dad serve their function within the family, likewise, children are a necessary part of the equation. That is why it is important for us to cherish and love each other. It is also "high time" for us to set aside our petty differences and/or "majoring on minor things." Life is short and good memories need to be established. There is a lot of love to give and God expects us to shower that love on each other every day!

Love is a beautiful thing and family are a beautiful blessing. A few years ago the Lord blessed me with a beautiful son and although being a mother for the first time has offered its many challenges and is a very tedious job, I bless the Lord for my son. He has made my life so much more rich and fulfilling. I love the opportunity the Lord gives me every day to wake up and be able to take care of my son. I have learned so much from him in terms of patience and he has taught me what unconditionally love looks like from a human standpoint.

And, I pray the Lord will bless and orchestrate his steps all the days of his life! I pray the Lord will shower him with his love and anointing from on high that will enable him in the future to work faithfully for his kingdom! I also pray the Lord will continue to bless and strengthen the both of us, so that we can be a strong and secure family unit that not only will be a wonderful blessing to each other but a wonderful blessing and light to the world!

Furthermore, my mother is close to my heart and although we don't get a chance to see each other that often, I love her dearly with all my heart and thank God for her imparting to me her wisdom, strength and faith. She is a God-fearing woman. She loves her family and is a very outspoken individual. If you don't want a "real answer" to life, then don't ask her, because she will tell you the truth! I look forward to our conversations and I thank God for her constant prayers and strong emotional support that has been a great help in times of distress. But, what I appreciated most of all is her faithfulness to doing God's work and being a powerful representation of Him.

For you to Ponder: When was the last time you called your mother, brother or other family member to check up on them? Call today. You make sure that you do your part regardless of what the other person does or doesn't do because "tomorrow isn't promised." Spend quality time together for memories are priceless and you can't get the time lost back!

Fire, God's Purifier

"But he knows the way that I take; when he has tested me, I will come
forth as gold (Job 23: 10, NIV)."

PRAISE GOD FOR THIS great opportunity to speak as an oracle and instrument for God's glory. I am writing this article as an encouragement to those who feel that they are suffering needlessly and have become discouraged along life's journey and their faith walk because things in their life appear that they are a series of unending trials and pains and hardships.

First of all, I want you to know that God loves you! And, yes, God sees what you are going through and you are not alone, for he promised to never leave you nor forsake you (Hebrews 13:5, NIV)." Trials and struggles in life are never fun to go through and because of the things that we endure in life, if we are not careful, it can cause us to question God's faithfulness and love for us. But regardless, God is faithful and loves us beyond our human comprehension. He loves us so much that he sent his son Jesus to atone for our sins (John 3:16, NKJV). And it is that same love that God has for his children that sometimes requires disciplinary action to reshape and mold us into the image of his son Jesus.

When we look at discipline although it is a very uncomfortable and painful process, the end result as the word of God clearly illustrates that "Afterwards there will be a peaceful harvest of right living for those who are trained in this way (Hebrews 12:11, NLT)."

This reminds me of a person that has resolved to be more proactive with healthy living and losing weight. In the beginning the whole process can be very overwhelming. The exercise regime is rigorous and sometimes the weight seems to take a while to come off. The person lifts heavy weights to work their muscles and many days, they feel the effects i.e. pain and sourness but regardless they have resolved to keep working out to produce the desired effect.

That is what God does with us when he is purifying us. His desire is to exercise our faith (Hebrews 11:1, Habakkuk 2:4, NLT) build our trust (Proverbs 3:5, NIV), flex spiritual muscles (I Timothy 4:8, NLT) and therefore produce in us spiritual growth and maturity in Christ (II Corinthians 13:9, Hebrews 13:21 and Colossians 2:10, NIV). So, don't get in the way of what God is doing in your life. It may be hard, you may feel like giving up and you may get tired but fight the good fight of faith, "looking unto Jesus which is the author and finisher of your faith (Hebrews 12:2, NKJV)."

As I conclude this article, it is my prayer that God will perform his work in all of us. Anything that God does isn't for our demise but for our ultimate good, even those hard places and difficult seasons in life that we may not understand. Be encouraged my sisters and brothers because God is going to be glorified through your pain and struggles. Hold onto his love, pray and seek him daily and know that "all things work together for good to them that love God, to them who are the called according to his purpose (Romans 8:28, KJV)" and be very confident in knowing "that he which hath begun a good work in you will perform it until the day of Jesus Christ (Philippians 1:6, KJV)."

For You to Ponder: God loves us and sometimes we need to be placed on "the potter's wheel again so that God can remold and reshape us as well as through the "fire of discipline and correction," so that God may purge our hearts, purge our motives and purge us so that can be spiritual transformed and equipped for his service.

God, the Only Way to Eternal Life

"I am the way, the truth and the life, No one comes to the Father except through me (John 14:6, NLT)."

As WE LOOK CLOSELY at our world today, it appears that many are drawing further and further away from God. Although many churches are being erected all around us and there seems to be no shortage of places to "fellowship" on any given Sunday, many people are still dying without God!

Contrary to the fact that we have many churches, denominations, religious organizations, pastors, or as we phrase it "men of God" or "women of God," we have not been as productive in our evangelistic efforts and/or spreading the Gospel of Jesus Christ to others. Sadly, many of us instead of being "salt and light" (Matthew 5:13-16, NKJV) and to be "separate" (II Corinthians 6:17, NKJV) from the world, have adopted the "world's mentality" (II Peter 2:15, NKJV) (Philippians 3:18, 19, NKJV) (II Corinthians 11:14, NKJV) and ideology of "appearance, works and prosperity focused" (Matthew 23:23-27, KJV). But, despite our philosophy of life, I am so glad to know who the true source is and that is God!

It is not with material things, money, relationships, or any other things this world has to offer. There is no true wholeness or peace outside of God and He is the only way to life eternal! Or as the Bible so eloquently exemplifies, "I come that they might have life and have it more abundantly (John 10:10, NKJV)."

Since it has been made evidently clear where our joy and peace comes from, I would be remiss if I didn't articulate ways in which we grow in relationship with God and therefore, have the privilege of inheriting eternal life through Him!

1. Although it is clear that we "all have sinned" and fallen short of God's glory (Romans 3:23, NKJV), God offers abundant life to all who desires it (John 10:10, NKJV).

2. Secondly, although we are deserving of death and punishment because of our sins, life is offered through Christ (Romans 6:23, John 3:16, John 10:28, I John 5:11).

3. Thirdly, even though we as people think that we have willpower and is in control of what we do, it isn't about "sin management" but about what Jesus does on our behalf to free us from the captivity of sin (Ephesians 2:9, NKJV)."

4. Furthermore, it is all about Jesus' death, burial and resurrection, all for our eternal benefit (Romans 5:8, I Corinthians 15:3-4, John 3:16, NKJV).

5. Also, we must recognize that Jesus is the only way to God and that there are no alternatives! (John14:6, I John 5:6-13).

6. Moreover, although that is the case, there are some "individual decisions" that we must make (John 1:12, Matthew 19:29, Leviticus 19:2, Isaiah 55:6, Hebrews 12:1-2, Matthew 16:24-26).

7. To add, "repentance" is key! (Matthew 3:2, Acts 3:19, Acts 17:30, Revelations 3:19, II Corinthians 7:1).

8. Likewise, placing faith in God is integral (Ephesians 2:8, NKJV) and making a lifelong commitment to him (Romans 10:9-10, 13, NKJV).

After you have made the commitment to live a spiritually transformed life, remember that that is just the beginning and that as a Christian and "walking according to the spirit and not according to the flesh," there are many spiritual disciples that must be evident in your daily life:

1. "Love the Lord your God" (Deuteronomy 6:5, KJV).

2. "Be Holy" (Leviticus 19:2, NKJV).

3. Keep God's commandments (Exodus 20:1-17, NKJV).

4. Obey Him (I Samuel 15:23, NKJV).

5. Operate in "Fruits of the Spirit" (Galatians 5:22, 23).

6. "New Man Character" (Colossians 3:12-17).

7. Love and Forgiveness Evident in Life and in relation to others (Leviticus 19:18, II Corinthians 2:7, Ephesians 4:32, Colossians 3:13, Hebrews 13:1, I John 4:7).

8. Study, Obey and Apply Scriptures to Daily Life (II Timothy 2:15, Joshua 1:18, II Timothy 3:16, II Peter 1:20, NKJV).

In conclusion, you should make it your aim to seek God wholeheartedly (Isaiah 55:6, NKJV) and draw closer to him. "Life isn't promised" (James 4:14, KJV) and no one knows when God will return (Matthew 24:36, NKJV). So, I implore you to "Be Ready" (Matthew 25:10, NKJV)! Don't allow the distractions of this world to hinder you from hearing from God and responding to his call, and, as a result, when he returns, you are left behind (Matthew 25:1-13, NKJV) (I Thessalonians 4:13-17, NKJV). "God loves you and I love you, will you come? He is available with his arms stretched wide open ready to receive you home!"

For You to Ponder: Surrendering your life to God is the best decision you will ever make!

God Will Fight For Us

"Then I prayed, hear us, our God, for we are being mocked (Nehemiah 4:9, NLT)."

PRAISE GOD FOR HIS indescribable love that he has bestowed upon us. It is always a refreshing to know undoubtedly that we have a heavenly father that loves us and is concerned about our wellbeing. It doesn't matter what we have to suffer or endure "on this side of life," "God is our refuge and our strength (Psalms 46:1, KJV)."

Although that is the case, we as people need to be aware that in life we are going to endure some struggles and hardships that we may not fully understand, life maybe overwhelming and perplexing at times and we may be battling unseen forces that we are not aware of but irrespective, God is there for he promised to "never leave us nor forsake us (Hebrew 13:5, NKJV)."

For example, as we look at Nehemiah chapter four specifically, we understand from our reading that Nehemiah and the people of Judah faced opposition regarding the rebuilding of the wall of Jerusalem. They were mocked and threatened but despite all that they encountered, they didn't cease their efforts and more importantly, they prayed and sought the help of the Lord.

As I read the Bible further and looked at the actions of Sanballat and how he tried to block and hinder God's people, I am reminded of how Satan tries to block us in every way and our desire to fulfill God's purpose and plan for our lives and, will use people, circumstances, or whatever he can to "throw us into confusion (v.8)," get our eyes off of God and keep us from multiplying and being effective for the kingdom of God.

But regardless, we have to continue to move forward just as Nehemiah and the people of Judah. It may appear that it may get harder and more difficult and that we seem so far from our goal i.e. "the workers are getting tired, and there is so much rubble to be moved (v.10.)," but that isn't the time to give up and throw in the towel but with the supernatural strength that is given by way of the Holy Spirit, Gird yourselves and prepare for battle and go out to win i.e. "So I placed armed guards behind the lowest parts of the wall in the exposed areas. I stationed the people to stand guard by families, armed with swords, spears and bows . . . Remember the Lord, who is great and glorious . . . Our God will fight for us (vs. 13, 20)."

And God will fight for you for "the battle isn't yours but the Lords" (I Samuel 17:47, NKJV). Oftentimes we as people wonder why we are not being victorious in our lives and things seem so out of alignment. The reason is because the battle isn't against tangible things or people but it is unseen forces in the spirit world (Ephesians 6:12, NIV).

The devil has lost his position in heaven because of pride and wanting what didn't belong to him and as a result, he is roaming the earth "seeking whom he may devour" (I Peter 5:8, NKJV). The devil's overall agenda and scheme is to hinder people from reaching their destination in life and ultimately their eternal destiny in Christ. He is furious and we as children of God are his primary target for destruction.

That is why we must always be "armored up" through prayer, time in God's presence and through his word which is the "sword of the spirit" (Ephesian 6:17, NIV). Because then and only then are we in position to fight competently in the spirit realm.

And finally, don't be surprised at the "fiery trials you are going through, as if something strange were happening to you. Instead be very glad for these trials make you partners with Christ in his suffering" (I Peter 4:13, 14, NKJV). In other words, the attack is coming but when it does, don't be baffled by it but know that that is the assurance that you are connected to the "true vine" (John 15:1, NIV) and are a part of the family of Christ and just as he is victorious so are you for "Greater is he that is in you than he that is in the world (I John 4:4, NKJV)."

For You to Ponder: Stop fighting battles that isn't yours to fight! Let God do what you can't and let him work it out for you in ways that is beyond your human logic or comprehension. God is omnipotent you are not, so let him have it!

Greed, Satan's Device to Destroy Mankind

"For the love of money is the root of all evil: which while some coveted after, they have erred from the faith, and pierced themselves through with many sorrows (I Timothy 6:10, KJV)."

LOOK AT OUR WORLD today and it appears that we are drawing further and further way from God. We have become a very materialistic society and it would seem from outward observation that our main objective in life is geared toward material and financial attainment. It also would appear that in our society, people would go to any "lengths," i.e. exploit themselves, compromise their relationship with God, deceive and manipulate other people, prostitute themselves, stay in unhealthy relationships or even go as far as to murder someone all correlated to greed. The Bible tells us emphatically, "That those who desire to be rich fall into temptation and a snare, and into many foolish and harmful lusts which drown men in destruction and perdition (I Timothy 6:9, NKJV)."

Satan's whole objective is to disconnect us from God and destroy us in the process. He will try anything and he realizes that in order for us to be able to take care of our basic necessities, it would help tremendously to have "money" (Ecclesiastes 10:19, NKJV). There is nothing wrong with money in general and your desire to be able to take care of your overall financial needs and that of your family. It is when you are so greedy for money that it drives you to commit crimes and hurt other people that places you on a downward path of destruction. I used to be very surprised at the levels of corruption that people would go to for money but, as I am aware of the "times" that we live in, nothing surprises me anymore. The world's point of view is "more, more, more." That is, do what you can, while you can, in any way that you can to acquire material things. That is why "self-help" books are so popular as well as many talk shows and even inspirational programs are successful because the emphasis is on prosperity.

Again, I am not trying to belittle anyone or minimize all their hard work and otherwise that they have done to accomplish what they have. What I am saying is that our focus should be more on the state of "our hearts" and our relationship with God than on the things of this world. Jesus expressively tells us to "seek first the kingdom of God and His righteousness, and all these things shall be added to you (Matthew 6:33, NKJV)." Jesus already knows our needs and if we make it our aim to be "kingdom focused" and not "self-focused" God will supply us with what we need at the "appointed time" (Habakkuk 2:3, NKJV). This world is full of greed and wickedness and we as people that are focused on serving God and being examples for him shouldn't adopt the "same mentality," as the world but be more like God and follow his direction for our lives.

We as God's children and those that are serving him shouldn't be greedy. The Bible states that those who are God's people and are called to serve him i.e. a bishop or otherwise, "shouldn't be "given to wine, not violent, not greedy for money, but gentle, not quarrelsome, not covetous (I Timothy 3:3, NKJV)." We are called to live holy.

As people of God we are to maintain a standard of righteous living that should be evident to the world and those all around us. Instead of adopting a mentality to "get, get, get," we should be "giving of ourselves, giving of our time and giving of our resources to help others and further the kingdom of God!

The "old man" (Ephesians 4:19, 22 NKJV) or sinful nature is in constant battle with the "new man" (Ephesians 4:23, 24, 32, NKJV) or the Holy Spirit. With this constant battle going on, the devil's desire in the interim is to distract us and get our focus off God. He doesn't care that we profess Christianity or say that we love God, all he wants to do is obliterate us! That why the Bible clearly states, "so are the ways of everyone who is greedy for gain; It takes away the life of its owners (Proverbs 1:19, NKJV)."

My pray is that we would all seek God and have a relationship with him. Nothing on this earth can satisfy us and bring fulfillment like a relationship with God. Anytime we look to anything or anyone else, we always falter and are greatly disappointed. God is our "refuge and strength" (Psalm 46:1, NKJV) and we can bring all our "petitions" (I John 5:14, 15, NKJV) and the things that we need to him as God passionately tells us to "cast all of our cares upon him for he cares for us (I Peter 5:7)." We don't have to compromise for the "devil's goods." What God has for "us is for us" and when the Lord gives us anything, there is "peace and joy" as a result (Proverbs 10:22, NKJV), not a guilt, shame or fear. Likewise, stay focused, keep your eyes on God and he promises you a great "future and an expected end" (Jeremiah 29:11, NKJV).

For You to Ponder: Money is not the way, Jesus is the way!

I Am Not Alright

(LIFE) IS A SERIES of "highs and lows," successes and failures, "hits and misses" and mountaintops and valleys low. But, whatever state that we as people may find ourselves in, those various transitions can have either a positive or negative effect on our perception of life. For example, in the Bible "Hannah was one of the wives of Elkanah. He loved Hannah with a special love, so much that he gave her a double portion of his livelihood (I Samuel 1:5)." But regardless of all that Elkanah did for Hannah to express his love for her, she was not alright. In actuality, "she was miserable, refused to eat and was in bitterness of soul because she was barren and couldn't have a child that she greatly desired (vs. 6, 7, and 10)."

Have you ever been in a "place" in your life whereas, it appeared that no matter what you did, how you prayed and believed, your situation seemed interminable. And doesn't it appear that at the most difficult times of your life when it is "now or never," never seems to come? Well, it is in times like these that we have to be authentic with ourselves and with God about how we are feeling. I know that many of you have been taught to "count it all joy in diver's temptations (James 1:2)." And, although that is true and the ways in which we should deal with life, God never intended for us to be "fake and phony" about our emotions and the challenges that we face in life.

Even Jesus when he was in the Garden of Gethsemane he expressed very raw emotions and was in great distress. "And being in great agony, He prayed more earnestly. Then His sweat became like drops of blood falling down to the ground (Luke 22:44)." We don't ever have to pretend with God. We don't have to lock our emotions on the inside and make ourselves sick trying to impress God as we do with people because he knows that we are fragile and fragmented and in need of only what he can provide. We go through this life searching and searching for what we feel will fulfill the void that is on the inside and nothing seems to be the answer.

43

God amidst all of your searching and scrambling is waiting with his arms stretched wide open waiting to embrace you and pour his love on you that can fulfill your longing soul. The woman went to the well in search of natural water not knowing that she was coming in contact with the "true living water" (John 4:10) which is God. Obviously she previously had been looking for "love in all of the wrong places" because "she had many different relationships with men" (John 4:18). Haven't we all been where she is? Even in our religious sectors or denominations we look for churches that appeals to our since of belonging and connection and when that church or pastor disappoints us in some way, we are quick to point out that they are the problem, when in actuality the problem is on the inside and that again we are not alright!

And, outward observation is not a clear or "sure fire" indicator that we are alright because I have seen many people that smile and say all the right things but, shortly thereafter you hear of them committing suicide or harming others. We really need God as our source of help and strength through difficult seasons and at all times in life. I know that there are times in my own life whereas, I feel as if I am pushed to the edge and can't take anymore. It is in these times and at all times I look to Jesus which is the "author and finisher of my faith (Hebrews 12:2)." He gives me what I need spiritually and through the works of his Holy Spirit to endure what normally I know would have taken me out and I know that if you seek his help and guidance in your life, he will do the same thing for you!

For You to Ponder: When life seems to be beyond what you can bear remember before you try to figure it out that God has already worked it out!

I am Who I Am

"Love who God created you to be because you are uniquely you!"-
Jennifer Workman

THIS ARTICLE IS DEDICATED to all people who have wrestled with "identity issues." People who have succumbed to the deceptions and lies of Satan and people that make them feel that who they are, are not enough. For those who look to the media, look to relationships, look to money, look to material things and all the "world's goods" searching for wholeness, when all along, true peace and satisfaction comes from God!

Yes, "a peace" as the Bible so eloquently expresses "that surpasses all understanding that will guard our hearts and minds through Christ Jesus (Philippians 4:7, NKJV)." We will never truly understand who we are apart from God because God is the orchestrator of all things. And, it is through pray and communication with the father and meditating on his word, is where we find the answers to who we are. For instance, "You made all the delicate, inner parts of my body and knit me together in my mother's womb. Thank you for making me so wonderfully complex! Your workmanship is marvelous-how well I know it (Psalm 139: 13, 14, NLT)." Now, as you contemplate this particular citation from scripture, does that sound like a person that doesn't have an identity? No, of course not! That sounds like a person that is undoubtedly special and an integral part of God's purpose and plan for the world.

You are who God created you to be and that is why you should never minimize your value and significance as a person. But, as you look at yourself, tell yourself, I am who I am because "Greater is he that is in me than he that is in the world (I John 4:4, NKJV)." I am who I am because God created me to be on this earth and to operate as an "ambassador for Christ" (Ephesians 6:20, NLT). I am who I am because no one can be who God has created me to be other than me and I am okay with that and have no desire to walk in "someone's shoes." God created all of us for a reason and if we can see ourselves the way that he sees us, then, there wouldn't be so many "identity issues" in the world i.e. men wanting to be women, women wanting to be men, people looking to celebrities lives as an example of how they should live, not realizing, many of them have their own issues and many things are not "always the way they appear in the media."

God loves us just the way that we are! We don't have to be taller, younger, richer, lighter, darker or anything else because all of those things are not important to God. God accepts us with our "flaws and all." People have a falsified idea of others and no one can live up to the world's depiction of humanity nor should they strive to do so. Because as a result, they will come out empty and defeated because it is an unrealistic view of life! My suggestion is to look to God! Know that God is the final authority in all things and that anything he does is not for our ultimate demise but for our ultimate good!

And, anytime you feel that you are receiving messages about who you are that are not in alignment with what God says about you, my suggestion is to read and study God's word. For in it, you have all the answers to who you are and all that plagues you in life. For example, in the Bible with the story of the "Samaritan woman at the well" (reference John chapter four). She obviously wrestled with identity issues and sought her value and significance in multiple relationships with men but it wasn't until she came into the presence of the "true living water," that she could find peace and meaning in life because Jesus was all that she truly needed. And, Jesus is all that you need to fill the void and ache that is in your heart. For the Bible states "Give all of your worries and cares to God, for he cares about you (I Peter 5:7, NLT)."

Also, as you read the word of God and spend time in God's presence, it gives you peace and confidence to know unequivocally without a "shadow of a doubt" who you are and consequently you can say with boldness and without reservation, "The Lord is my light and my salvation so why should I be afraid? The Lord is my fortress, protecting me from danger, so why should I tremble? Though a mighty army surrounds me, my heart will not be afraid. Even when I am attached, I will remain confident (Psalm 27:1, 3, NLT)."

For You to Ponder: Love who God created you to be because you can only be you and no one else!

Itching Ears

"For the time will come when they will not endure sound doctrine; but after their own lusts shall they heap to themselves teachers, having itching ears (II Timothy 4:3, KJV)."

"PRAISE GOD FOR HIS uncompromising word, my prayer is that this article will permeate the hearts of those that read it, convict those that need convicting and most importantly bring about spiritual transformation in the hearts of all that behold it, in Jesus name."

As we take a close look at our world today, it is quite evident that we live in a time where as people need God in their lives more than ever before. Although people are excelling in their educational, business and other "societal pursuits," many are still without God and many that seemed to have had a good relationship with the heavenly father, is drawing further away from him, following after the "deceitfulness of riches" and the "cares of life" (Mark 4:19, BSB)."

And, that same "mindset" have infiltrated our churches and religious organizations disguising itself as "the prosperity gospel." I am in no way trying to "bash" anybody and this article is not intended for that purpose but, it is intended to expose the traps and wiles of the Devil. Today the "prosperity gospel" seems to be at the forefront of all that is pontificated in today's churches as well as in the world as a whole.

Having stated that, let's go a little deeper "shall we." The bible talks about people having "itching ears." It goes on to say that people (I'm paraphrasing), place leaders in position of authority to tell them what they want to hear to tickle their ears. Many people would much rather hear that the "Lord will bless you if you give, turn around three times and say money cometh," than, "you need to repent of your sins, for the kingdom of God is at hand" (Matthew 3:2, NKJV). But, it is that same truth of the word of God and not a lie that is going to truly set them free.

I don't know about anyone else but I would much rather hear the truth than a lie. For instance, in a relationship with a husband and a wife, the wife asks the husband how the dress she has recently purchased looks on her and without deliberation, he tells her something to make her feel good although the dress is not "figure flattering" and makes her look fat. Although no one is really being affected by what he stated, a "lie is simply a lie!" But what bears "heavy weight" is what we are being feed every day and if what we are being feed everyday isn't the truth but a lie, we need to really check the source and ask God to help us to receive the "word of truth" with gladness, whether is it what we want to hear or not because in the totality of it all, it is our souls that are at stake!

So, I implore you that in all that you do, seek God. Chase after him with all that is in you, for he is near and his arms are opened to you because everything on this "side of life" will perish but the word of God remains forever. Don't allow the lure of riches, the deception of the enemy and selfish ambition hinder you from moving forward in God and him leading and orchestrating your life as he sees fit. For as the Bible emphatically states that "God is coming back again" and my prayer is that we all will be ready for his great coming so that we will be able to hear him say "Well Done (Matthew 25:23, KJV)."

For You to Ponder: Seek to know that truth from God's word, even those things that make you say "ouch" "For the word of God is alive and active. Sharper than any double-edged sword, it penetrates even to dividing soul and spirit, joints and marrow; it judges the thoughts and attitudes of the heart (Hebrew 4:12, NIV)."

It's Mine

Do nothing out of selfish ambition or empty pride, but in humility
consider others more important than yourselves. Each of you should
look not only to your own interests, but also to the interests of others
(Philippians 2:3-4, NKJV)."

I HOPE AND PRAY this article will be enlightening and thought-provoking
for every reader. I pray that everyone as a result of reading this article, will
be mindful of the ways in which we deal with each other and know that
God has gifted, anointed and blessed all of us to make a contribution to the
world and we don't need to manipulate one another, deceive one another
or power-posture to have anything in life because what God intends for us
to have, we will have it, for the "Lord promised that he would supply all of
our needs according to his glorious riches, which have been given to us in
Christ Jesus (Philippians 4:19, NLT)."

First of all, before I proceed any further, I wanted to ask to the question, how many of you have children? If you like myself have one child or
even ten children, you are aware that children are born with a selfish nature.
Parents spend countless years teaching children the importance of sharing
with others and although that is the case, their children still wrestle with
each other for toys and possessions, as they articulate to each other boisterously "you can't have it the toy is mine." Although it may be humorous to
witness children reacting that way, it isn't funny to see two adults acting in
like manner for the Bible tells us "when I was a child, I spoke and thought
and reasoned as a child. But when I grew up, I put away childish things (I
Corinthians 13:11, NLT)."

I recently had the opportunity to read "Daily Devotional: The Word
For You Today" booklet created by Riverland Hills Baptist church and was
blown away by its contents and I am going to reference it today as it is

very applicable to what I am trying to articulate to every reader. One of the devotionals that I read was entitled "The Spirit of Diotrephes." In the opening portion of the devotional, it pointed out that, "some people are so insecure and easily threatened that they feel a need to tear down anyone they perceive as a competitor."

As I continued to read, the devotional referenced "Diotrephes" in (III John: 9-10, NLT). It highlighted "Diotrephes as one of the New Testament church leaders." For those of us that spend time in the word of God and are acquainted with Diotrephes, we understand that when John indicated to Diotrephes that he had some talented traveling teachers come and speak at his church, instead of the appropriate response which would be to receive the "men of God" with open arms recognizing they are doing the work of the Lord, as the Bible suggests, Diotrephes treated them contemptuously. He went as far as to spew evil accusations against the men of God, he refused to welcome them and when that wasn't enough, he went as far as to tell others not to help them and, when other people tried to help them, they were threatened with being put out of the church. Now, does that remind you of yourself at one point in time or your children's behavior when they don't get what they what? I would say yes for I have seen it represented in my own actions along the way and I have seen it manifested in my child's behavior at different times as well.

When you read and study the Bible, one thing becomes extremely evident and that is, "that there is nothing new under the sun (Ecclesiastes 1:9, NKJV)." As it was back then with Diotrephes and the church, so it is today in all relationships, churches and businesses. Just like the illustration I used earlier with children having a selfish nature and not wanting to share with others, that is likewise how many people relate to each other, they power-posture, manipulate, scheme and otherwise because in actuality they are acting like Diotrephes and the children and saying "It's mine."

That is the ultimate reason why many relationships are destroyed because of the spirit of "Diotrephes" in operation in many people. Someone is insecure and threatened by someone's success, education, physicality, qualifications and experience, and, as a result, they try to block someone's progress. Whether it is a church and people scheming and power-posturing for positions and recognition, whether it is a business establishment and those in leadership, trying to hire people for their company but feeling threatened by their qualifications, throws away the applicants resume without giving them a "second thought" or taking the easy way out and sending them a rejection letter and stating that "they are not the right fit for the job" or whether it is, as we see on television with various candidates running for President, the constant borough of insults, backbiting and "child's play" at work amongst the people, the reality of it all, is that the spirit of Diotrephes is masking itself being these responses. To add, John expressed his displeasure with all that Diotrephes was doing in (III John 11, NLT) he stated that "Dear friend, don't let this bad example influence you. Follow only what is good. Remember that those who do good prove that they are God's children, and those that do evil prove that they don't know God."

My prayer is that God will enable us through the work of his Holy Spirit, to humble ourselves and work together in the unity of Christ, no matter what level we are on. For we never accomplish anything by trying to tear others down to build ourselves up! When people operate in slanderous and deceptive ways against each other with the intent to hurt others to elevate themselves, they, as the devotional exemplifies, "are indulging the work of the Devil!"

For You to Ponder: "If you have two shirts, give one to the poor. If you have food, share it with those who are hungry (Luke 3:11, NKJV)."

Jesus Is Coming, Will You Be Ready?

"Look, I come like a thief! Blessed is the one who stays awake and
remains clothed, so as not to go naked and be shamefully exposed
(Revelation 16:15, NIV)."

THANK GOD FOR ANOTHER opportunity to be an instrument used for his
glory, I pray that this article blesses every reader, penetrate the hearts and
consequently causes someone to surrender their lives to the Lord and
choose to follow him.

As I look around me every day, I am constantly aware of the brevity
of life. As a child is birthed into this world at any given moment, the same
goes for a life that is taken away. We didn't come on this earth to stay; we are
just sojourners on this path of what we call life. Yet, we go about our daily
lives as if we have all the time in the world not aware that we could be here
today and gone tomorrow. I know we don't like to talk much about death
but dying is inevitable. We can't bypass it! We can eat healthy, exercise, take
various supplements for health and although all of those things are good
yet "No one can live forever; all will die. No one can escape the power of the
grave (Psalm 89:48, NLT)."

Now, ponder in your mind for a moment, if you know that life is short
and we didn't come on this earth to stay, then what do we have to look forward to? Well, I am glad you asked. If you have relationship with God and
have surrendered your life fully to him, you have heaven to look forward to
and spending eternity with God but if you reject the Father and seek to live
on your own disconnected from him, there is another place that is prepared
for those that reject God and that place is hell. Yes, hell, it is real just as
heaven is real. Don't ever let anyone deceive you and make you feel that
anything specified in the Bible is false because they are leading you astray. I
urge you to read it and study it for yourself and you will find that Hell isn't

a myth it is real! "For God did not spare even the angels who sinned. He threw them into hell, in gloomy pits of darkness, where they are being held until the Day of Judgment (II Peter 2: 4, NLT)."

Jesus is coming back again and when he returns, he is coming for a prepared people. It is never too late to get it right. Please people don't put it off because tomorrow isn't promised. Don't be like the "foolish virgins that didn't have oil and when the bridegroom came they weren't ready (Matthew 25:1-13, NKJV)." God loves you and it isn't his desire that anyone be destroyed, but wants everyone to repent (II Peter 3: 9, NLT)" but you have to make the choice to follow him! So, my question to you is "will you be ready," if Jesus came back today? If not, then the time is now and hear is how you can begin, say this prayer with me:

> "Heavenly Father, I come before you today asking for your forgiveness of all my sin. I acknowledge you as my Lord and Savior and that you sent Jesus to die for my sin. I can't live my life without you and I ask you to come into my life, clean me up, transform me and enable me through the power of your Holy Spirit to walk uprightly before you and live a surrendered life to you. Create in me a clean heart and renew a right spirit in me and help me to love you with all my heart, soul and mind and love my neighbors as myself in Jesus name, Amen!"

There are many angels in heaven rejoicing that you made the decision to give your life to the Lord. May I add that it is the best decision that you have ever made. Now ask the Lord through the power of the Holy Spirit to enable you to live a life that is pleasing in his sight and move forward in Jesus name. Again, time is short and no man knows when Jesus is going to return but regardless, it is always helpful to make sure that you are ready. God loves us and gave his only son for us because he doesn't want anyone to perish but have the opportunity to inherit eternal life (John 3:15-16, NLT)." And life is found only through Jesus for he is the way, the truth and the life, no one come through the Father except through him (John 14: 6, NKJV)."

To add, I want you to be mindful that living a sanctified life and one surrendered to God puts you on the devil's hit list. Remember he lost his place in glory and it is his desire that no man be able to experience what he has and have relationship with God. So, living as a Christian you must be armored up at all times for the Bible tells us that we should "Put on all of God's armor so that we will be able to stand firm against all strategies of the devil. For we are not fighting against flesh and blood enemies, but against evil rulers and authorities of the unseen world, against mighty powers in this dark world, and against evil spirits in the heavenly places (Ephesians 6:11-12, NLT)." So, ways in which you "armor yourself up" is by spending quality time with the Lord in prayer, spending time reading and studying his word and meditation and reflection in his presence. Because time in God's presence and filling ourselves up with his word enables us to fight competently in the Spirit against every force, power and demon of hell that tries to fight against us as a children of God.

In conclusion, Jesus is coming soon. As we look at our world and everything that is transpiring around us, God is likely to come at any time. For example, the Bible expressively states "But the day of the Lord will come as unexpectedly as a thief (II Peter 3:10, NLT)" so it behooves us to be ready. And, For the Lord himself will come down from Heaven with a commanding shout, with the voice of the archangel, and with the trumpet call of God. First the Christians who have died will rise from their graves. Then, together with them, we who are still alive and remain on the earth will be caught up in the clouds to meet the Lord in the air (I Thessalonians 4:16-17, NLT)." I implore all of us to make sure that we are ready when Jesus returns!

For You to Ponder: "Be Ready!"

Jesus Loves Me

"For God so loved the world, that he gave his only begotten Son, that
whosoever believeth in him should not perish, but have everlasting life
(John 3:16, NKJV)."

I WAS RECENTLY AT a local park and observed many children playing glee-
fully with each other but one child particularly caught my attention and
that child's name was Charlie. From observation, Charlie is a rambunc-
tious, creative and impressionable young boy and although Charlie was
playing and having fun with the other kids, he would frequently stop and
walk over to his father sitting on a nearby park bench and would ask the
question "Daddy would you like to play?" The dad smiles at his toddler
son and replies "No" but I will watch you from a safe distance. The little
boy looks at his father and smiles, then asks "Daddy do you love me?" The
dad surprised to hear the question responses enthusiastically, "Charlie, you
know that I do!" Then the father embraces and kisses his son and lets him
go back and play with the other children.

As I watched from a distance, I thought that was the most precious
sight to behold and at that moment, it caused me to recall the song "Jesus
Loves Me." As a child I remember the lyrics to that song "Jesus loves me this
I know for the Bible tells me so." Although that song is etched in the hearts
of many children around the world and they know it verbatim, I wonder
if many of us as human beings are like Charlie that asks Jesus the question
"Do you love me," then it is quite evident that he does.

How many of us have allowed our circumstances, broken relationships and other difficulties in life to obscure our vision of our loving Heavenly Father and caused us to view him from our human lenses and finite
understanding. God is not like man! For the Bible expressively tells us that
we can trust God i.e. "Trust in the Lord with all of your heart and lean not

to your own understanding, in all of your ways acknowledge him and he will direct your paths (Proverbs 3:5, NKJV)." We can trust that God loves us, that God cares for us and that God knows what is best for us. "For God is our refuge, a very present help in the time of trouble (Psalm 46:1, NKJV) and he gave his one and only son to atone for our sins (John 3:16, NKJV).

When we understand the ultimate price Jesus paid for our sins, then we understand his depth of love for all mankind and that no matter how we feel or what we encounter in life, he is always with us for he emphatically states in the Bible that "I will never leave you nor forsake you (Hebrews 13:5, NKJV)." If ever there is any contemplation in your mind of Jesus's love for you, let me highlight a few biblical citations for your encouragement and learning:

1. (John 3:16) For God so love the world that he gave his only begotten son.

2. (Hebrews 13:5) I will never leave you nor forsake you.

3. (Isaiah 43:2) When you go through deep waters, I will be with you . . .

4. (I John 4:4) Greater is he that is in me than he that is in the world.

5. (John 11:36) See how much he loved him . . .

In conclusion, it is my prayer that you will let these scriptures permeate your mind and take root in your hearts and always be reminded of Jesus's great love for you. All of us have a special place in God's heart and are special in his sight i.e. "For whoever touches you touches the apple of his eye (Zechariah 2:8)." God is concerned about all people and "desires that none perish but that all have eternal life" (II Peter 3:9, NKJV) and that is his purpose for sending Jesus to die for us and that is why he is so patient with us, for he knows that we are imperfect people and that "we come from the dust" (Genesis 2:7, NKJV).

Hear the totality of the matter, Jesus loves you! Don't go through life feeling like you are alone because you are not alone because Jesus is always near. My prayer is that you will seek his will and purpose for your life and be transformed by his power and thus know the unconditional love that God has for you!

For You to Ponder: God loves you greatly. Don't let anyone deceive you into thinking that no one loves you. God paid a great price on the cross for all of mankind and that includes you!

Laughter Medicine for the Soul

"Medicine is needed but laughter is absolutely indispensable"-Jennifer
Workman

As a child I consistently was told to smile and laugh because laughter is
good for you. I found biologically when you smile and/or laugh, you positively alter the functioning of your body and you feel a sense of euphoria. I
look around me all the time and see many people that look so sad or have
a disgruntle look on their faces. From outward observation, they appear to
be so unhappy and dissatisfied with their lives. You would never know if
"life" is as difficult as it seems, unless you sit down and have a heart to heart
conversation with them.

I love to smile and laugh about the "mundane" types of situations because it is "truly medicine for the soul." Laughing can truly change your
entire day even if you're having a "bad day," try laughing at yourself or
thinking of something humorous and "you won't stay in that condition
for long." I would go as far as to ask you to try that exercise at least once
every day that would improve your overall physical, mental and emotional
health. I know we as people are constantly inundated with negative news
coverage about the economy, gas prices and various other world issues but,
regardless, make it your aim to laugh and live every day to the fullest despite circumstances all around you! No one has the power to change what is
going on all around us but God and we can release everything in his capable
hands.

Furthermore, laughter is an important part of the process. Sadness,
bitterness, and other negative emotions makes us sick on the inside because
our bodies weren't created to adequately function in a constant state of up-
heaval and emotional unstableness. God cares about our overall well-being
and wants us to be happy, laugh and live victorious lives. He knows that

we are imperfect people and that we oftentimes make many mistakes that challenges our overall health and wellbeing but regardless, he cares for us deeply.

So, as you go through your day, envision it as being a wonderful day. Why? Because what "you perceive is what you believe!" If you envision yourself as victorious and see every day positively, then you will find many reasons to laugh and have a wonderful day. On the other hand, if you view life as a series of struggles, disappointments and failures, you will manifest that internally and externally. So I implore you to "laugh, laugh, laugh and again I say laugh!"

For You to Ponder: Laugh again!

Let Your Faith Move You to Heights Unattainable in Christ

WHAT IS FAITH? THE Bible expressively tells us that "faith is the substance of things hoped for, the evidence of things not seen (Hebrews 11:1-NKJV)." In other words, regardless of whether you are physically or visibly able to acquire something, you stand firmly believing that unequivocally it is going to happen. Faith is not to be underestimating and although God has given us all access to faith, many of us don't utilize it productively in various areas of our lives. Many of us express passionately our faith in God but "life" usually happens and really tests to the core what our belief truly is! It is easy to say I trust God when we go through tests in our lives that seem to be "short lived" and really don't affect us to the core of our being. But, it is another thing to go through a "wilderness experience" for an extensive period of time, whereas, it seems to matter how much you pray, fast, what decisions you make or otherwise, it has the appearance that things are unchangeable. Do you still believe and trust God in those instances?

It appears to be those "elongated occurrences" in our lives that really troubles us and really exposes what is truly in our hearts and how we truly feel about God. Some people say that they love God and is faithful to him but when trouble comes, it is those same people that "curse" God and fault him for the situations that arises in their lives; they have completely thrown "faith out the window" and is now playing the "blame game." God doesn't want us just to love and trust him in good times, but he requires that same level of faith and trust even in our darkest moments of life. It is at these "dark moments" that we should affirm our faith through the word of God and speak "life not death" (Proverbs 18:21-NKJV) to our situation.

As it relates to our faith, we need to be like a long distant runner. A long distant runner is a focused individual. He or she comes onto the field with focus and determination to win the race that is set before them. Although they have trained and prepared themselves, they are aware that there may be obstacles that may occur in the process i.e. bad weather, time delays, physical injuries or otherwise. But, although that may or may not be the case, they are ready! As they make their mark, they are looking ahead. They are not focused on what or who is beside or behind them. They start and run the race with such grace and tenacity and sometimes in the process, they may start to feel the fatigue of running for a long time but they don't allow those pains and distractions to hinder their progress; they just keep running until they reach their destination.

Likewise, that is how every person should be when it comes to their faith in God. It is firm and unshakeable. Life and everything that comes with it can't impede their progress because their trust isn't in self but in God. Satan doesn't want us to have that "conquering mentality" because he knows that, that is the way we grow in God and is able to reach those unattainable heights of faith. But, faith requires a continual press. Press against fear, press against circumstances, press against "naysayers," press against obstacles and even those negative thoughts that seem to dominate your psyche and believe as the long distant runner do that you will win. It is at this point that God enables you to move forward and endure things that you never thought that you would have been able to endure and thus you grow and mature spiritually and increase in your faith. So, my brothers and sisters, "Hang on in there" and trust God in all areas of your life for he has promised to "never leave you nor forsake you (Hebrews 13:5-NKJV)" and that is what faith is and that is what will take you to heights unattainable in Christ!

For You to Ponder: Let your faith grow, trust God!

Letting go of the past, Looking towards the Future

"But one thing I do, forgetting those things which are behind and reaching forward to those things which are ahead (Philippians 3:13, NKJV)."

LIFE IS A SERIES of "ups and downs," successes and failures, rewards and demotions. But whatever state that we as people may find ourselves in, we can take solace in knowing that God is in control. God isn't just in control when everything is "well" and we always get what we desire in life but, God is also sovereign whether "good or bad" for He promises "to never leave us nor forsake us" (Hebrews 13:5, NKJV).

That fact is very hard for many people to internalize in times of extreme difficulty, especially when they have experienced hardship for an extensive period of time. For example, it is easy for a runner to endure a race if it is a sprint and he/she starts and finishes quickly. But, it is more challenging for the runner if they have to run a great distance. Why? Because distant running takes training of the mind and body to be able to persevere and win. Similarly if we as people are going to win in life, we must adopt the same mentality as the distant runner.

Not only should we strive to press in our race of life, but the ways in which we do this is by letting go of our past failures, mistakes and disappointments and move forward. Some people are stuck in life because they choose to keep dwelling on the past. Whether it is a broken relationship, job loss, bad financial decision or likewise, they just won't let go! They blame everyone and everything else for their problems and don't effectively deal with their varying issues through prayer, confession and self-analysis. As a result, they are left miserable, defeated and unhappy.

This isn't God's desire for our lives. He wants us to be free, "for who the son sets free is free indeed (John 8:36, NKJV)." We can wholeheartedly make the choice to be free or to stay encapsulated by bondage. "I choose to be free!" Freedom feels so much better than bondage! And, ways in which we can free ourselves from the snare and entrapment of bondage and sin is when we ask for forgiveness from God, choose to forgive ourselves for the past mistakes and poor decisions that we have made and also choose to forgive others for their wrong and mistreatment towards us.

We also free ourselves when we choose to view life positively and not negatively. We absolutely free ourselves through the powerful working of the Holy Spirit that indwells within our hearts and that is able to cleanse us inside outside, spiritually transform our lives and thus give us joy, peace and happiness in Jesus. So, why don't you make up your mind to "let go and let God?" I know that this sounds like a cliché but it is truth. I doesn't matter what you have done or where you are presently because God is able to take all of your problems and mistakes and turn it around for your good!

Yes, for "your good" and most importantly that God would be glorified! If there is ever any contemplation in your mind regarding this fact, I urge you to take a look at the word of God. Because in it, you will find innumerable examples of people in the Bible that once lived, made mistakes and regardless of their past was able to move forward into the destiny God orchestrated for their lives. One excellent example being David. David made the terrible mistake of committing adultery with Bathsheba and thereafter, having her husband killed to cover up his sin (II Samuel 11:1-27, NKJV)." Even though David did something so foolish and incomprehensible, it didn't thwart the plan of God for his life. Yes, it is to be dully noted that he didn't bypass the consequences of his sin but, once he cried out to God for forgiveness, repented and confessed his sin, he was able to move forward and God blessed him (II Samuel 12:1-25, NKJV).

And, that is what we must do to be able to move forward in our lives. Bring every sin, mistake and misstep to our Heavenly Father. God knows what is best for us and he also knows how to transform our lives. Again, there is nothing that we can do to change the past but, God can through his transformative power, give us a bigger, brighter and better future (Jeremiah 29:11, NKJV).

For You to Ponder: The past is the past, let it go and move forward for God has a greater future in store for you!

My Best Life, Yet

HAVE YOU EVER ASKED yourself "what do I expect from life" and have I been created for a "greater purpose?" If you haven't found what you have been created for just yet, that doesn't give you any reason to not live your best life and here are various ways in which you can do so:

1. View life optimistically and not pessimistically. The bible states expressively "For as he thinks in his heart so is he (Proverbs 23:7, NKJV)." "You are what you believe." If you believe that you are going to succeed in life, live every day to the fullest and have a great attitude, then that is what you are going to attract.

2. Take time to utilize your God-given abilities to help and bless others because nothing is more rewarding and satisfying than giving of "oneself" to help others. In doing so, we are truly representing ourselves as children of God. "Just as the Son of Man didn't come to be served but to give His life as a ransom for many (Matthew 20:28, NKJV)."

3. Prioritize time to cultivate good relationships with family, friends and others. "We are not an island of ourselves," and we cannot function adequately alone because we need each other. As you go through life, it is always refreshing to have good relationships with others to help you celebrate your successes as well as be there for you in your difficult "seasons" of life.

4. Most important of all, relationship with God is the ultimate way of living your best life yet! No matter what you accomplish in life, if you are not connected with the "true source," you will not be afforded the privilege of living life to fullest extent because God is the source of all joy and peace. I would much rather live life with God at the head of my life, than without him! Every day, people look to money, careers,

and relationships to give their lives meaning and significance, to be greatly disappointed. Why? Because who they are as a whole is connected to God and not to this world!

Overall, these are the ways in which "we can live our best life yet!"

For You to Ponder: Take life by the wings and soar as high as you can, you have been given only one life to live

Prevailing Prayer

WHY DON'T WE PRAY more? If we really understood the powerful impact of prayer, shouldn't that be a constant in our lives, as much, or even more so than, eating or drinking? Prayer is absolutely indispensable in today's society. The media is overly inundated with stories of unending homicides, innumerable theft, widespread diseases and all other categories of sin and destruction. More than ever before, we need to pray, and "I mean pray" for the Bible tells us that the effectual fervent prayer of the righteous man availeth much (James 5:16, AKJV)."

Prayer changes things! If we want to see change in our world, in our lives and in the lives of our loved ones, we have to incorporate prayer daily in our lives. Prayer is the "open pathway" to the Father and a tremendous "stress reliever." No where can you go and truly expose yourself intimately without judgment but with God. "It's not like you are telling Him something that he doesn't already know" because God knows everything about you!

I am thankful for a wonderful connection with my Heavenly Father through prayer. There have been countless times in my life whereas, I felt that in the various struggles of life that no one really understood my pain but it has always been so refreshing and therapeutic to come humbly in the presence of God and to cast my cares before him (I Peter 5:7, NKJV). God has never left my side (Hebrews 13:5 NKJV) and have remained true to his word!

Prayer is another way to seek the Lord for wisdom and direction in life. Many people feel that they are the "orchestrator" of everything that transpires in their lives and thus don't seek the Lord for help and as a result, they make many costly and undoable mistakes. We need the awesome and competent hands of the creator to lead us and help us to make Godly and wise decisions in our lives. For the word of God tells us empathically "that men always ought to pray and not loose heart (Luke 18:1)."

Furthermore, prayer is an effective tool to utilize against Satan. Satan knows the powerful effects of prayer. That is why he creates multiple distractions to try and hinder our prayer life. But the Bible states clearly that "we should give ourselves to prayer (Psalm 109:4, NKJV)." Prayer encourages us and empowers us in our faith walk. Once we pray, believe and begin to speak in faith to our situations, God strengthens us in the process and enables us to stand firm trusting him fully to bring us through victorious!

So, I implore you by the mercies of God and as a faithful servant of the Lord to pray. "Pray when you feel like it and pray when you don't!" God is waiting to hear from you. It doesn't matter whether you are a believer or not, God desires to hear from you. Make up in your mind that no matter what you have in life, no matter how you feel and no matter the devil's schemes that he utilizes to hinder you, that you are going to prevail or press through in prayer because whatever you need whether it is peace, joy, love or happiness, it is all found through God and in communication with Him!

For You to Ponder: Prayer is powerful so take time to pray for someone today.

Simply Single and Loving It

"OH THE DREADED WORD single." Is that what it sounds like when you talk to certain people?" They have such a misguided interpretation of what single-ness is all about, therefore they impose their views upon everyone in terms of, what they characterize "singleness" to be. And sadly, more often than not, the communication that they give to others is very judgmental and critical, often times making a single person believe that there is something wrong with them because they are single or somehow they are incomplete.

I remember attending seminary school several years and ago and having the privilege to meet and communicate with so many diverse groups of people both racially, denominationally and socially. At that time, I would hear many married couples as well as single couples give their views on marriage and singleness. Frequently, more often than I would have liked to hear, I heard many married couples say to single men and women, "so when are you getting married?," "do you desire to have children and if so, you know your clock is ticking?," "why are you not married?," "It is best to be married in ministry and working for God, so that you will not be tempted to sin," and "marriage overall is better than being single." "Really?" This kind of "one-sided" jargon left many singles feeling somewhat disgruntle and discouraged.

To add, in the seminary school, there were very few organizations, clubs, and/or functions that catered to singe people in general. I was single at that time and myself, as well as, other singles questioned this issue. People need to recognize that there is nothing wrong with being single. Single doesn't mean that you are lacking anything or anyone. It doesn't mean that you are incomplete and it doesn't mean that you are desperate for companionship.

Before we can bring our "best selves" to a relationship or otherwise, we need to embrace singleness and be content with who we are and we need to live life to the fullest and take life by the "wings and soar." Single people need to love themselves completely and they need to see themselves as special and as a part of the divine plan of God! Single people need to recognize that they are more loyal to the kingdom of God and able to do more for his glory. The bible expressively states "He who is unmarried cares for the things of the Lord-how he may please the Lord. But he who is married cares about the things of the world-how he may please his wife (I Corinthians 7:42, NKJV)."

So, as an encouragement to all single people, I, as a "mouth piece" for the Lord, implore you again to:

1. Love who God created you to be in "all of your singleness."

2. Embrace live and life it to the fullest.

3. Don't let anyone make you feel that you are insignificant just because you aren't married.

4. Singleness is a blessing because it allows you to be able to do more for the Kingdom of God.

5. Let God transform your life through the power of the Holy Spirit, make you whole and thus, help you to be the best person you can be!

I have seen over the years many singe people doing great things for God and in the world as a whole. Why? Because they are simply single and loving it. They are loving who God created them to be and they are loving the many opportunities that they have been given to do well in the world and help other people. They don't see being singe as negative but positive and their lives are representative of this fact.

For You to Ponder: Love yourself, love who God created you to be and live a purpose driven life!

Strengthen My Hands

"Now therefore, O God, strengthen my hands (Nehemiah 6:9, NKJV)."

ALL THAT I AM and all that I will ever be is because of God's love, grace and mercy that is unfathomable towards me. He is my strength and he directs me on this overwhelming journey of life. I understand without reservation that "God is my refuge and strength a very present help in the time of trouble" (Psalms 46:1, NKJV) and if I try to attempt anything in life without consulting with him first for wisdom, knowledge, discernment and direction, I am susceptible to a great fall and devastation (Proverbs 16:18, NKJV). So, I have resolved in my life that God is my orchestrator, God is my shield and God is my help. It is not my education, it is not the money in my banking account, it is not my family nor my friends, God is my source in life. He is the reason why I live, move and have my being (Acts 17:28, NKJV).

As we take a look at Nehemiah the sixth chapter, Nehemiah adopted this same mentality. He understood the sovereignty of God and he understood his need for God to direct him in all phases of his life. For instance, when Nehemiah and the people of God were rebuilding the wall and they found themselves being ridiculed, threatened and harassed by the enemy (refer to Nehemiah chapter four), Nehemiah knew the value of prayer and talking to the Lord i.e. "Now therefore, O God, strengthen my hands (Nehemiah 6:9, NKJV)." Nehemiah knew in order for him to be successful and build despite opposing forces, the only way it could be done is through Godly intervention and every person associated with the building working together.

Nehemiah and the people had the challenge of rebuilding the wall with limited materials (reference Nehemiah chapter four). If they would have looked to themselves, listened to the threats and negativity of others, then they would have ceased their efforts but they did not. I believe in order for us to overcome adversities and trials of life, it takes incongruous trust and faith in God to continue to move forward despite what we don't have and it also gives God the opportunity to show himself strong on our behalf.

Nehemiah, although he worked and had people working around him, He needed help from the Lord. We as people need also to recognize our need for God. Yes, we may have money, connections and otherwise but, nothing will happen unless God moves in the mist of things for us. Nehemiah in the mist of all that he encountered asked the Lord to help him. When I think of this I believe what he was asking God to do was empower him to do what he couldn't do within his own strength. When we have God as our guide and spearheading every direction of our lives, I don't care what adversities that we may encounter, what limitations, and what hindrances or otherwise, God will help us to overcome and be victorious in the process.

I don't know about you but I need God to strengthen my hands. I need God to lead me in all things, show me the way, and give me wisdom, understanding and direction in life. I know with his help I am assured victory in the end. I implore you again in all things talk to the Lord in prayer. For in conversation with the Lord, you will receive clear guidance and instruction for life. It is very risky thinking that we as human beings with our "finiteness," knows what is best for ourselves other than the omniscient and infinite God. As you ask him to "strengthen your hands," trust that he knows what is best and is leading you to where he would have for you to go which is far better than what you can fathom as a human being. And, always remember no matter what that "all things work together for good, to them that love the Lord and are called according to his purpose (Romans 8:28, NKJV)."

For You to Ponder: What are you trying to accomplish today. Whatever it maybe recognize that "little is much" in the hands of the Lord. Place everything on the "altar of prayer" and trust God to enable you to accomplish through his power, great exploits and feats in Jesus name. Write out goals and aspirations, give yourself a set deadline to finish and pray, pray, pray about every transition.

The Inner Man Verses the Outer Man: What Does God Look At?

"People judge by outward appearance, but the Lord looks at the heart (I Samuel 16:7, NLT)."

WHAT DO YOU SEE when you see yourself in the mirror? Do you like what you see? I do, although I am constantly, as a woman, inundated with images in the media of beauty and what traits, characteristics and physical attributes makes a woman beautiful and although the majority of the time I am in disagreement with the media, that is how the world system functions. But if we were to look at the truth and not a lie, the Bible is very clear that although we as people have a tendency to judge each other based on "outward appearance" (I Samuel 16:7, NLT) and tangible things, God has a very different view of mankind.

Take for instance in the Bible when Saul lost his place as King. Samuel went to Jesse to choose one of his son's as the next king in Saul's place. When Samuel came and saw one of the son's, he responded as many of us respond towards each other based on outward appearance i.e. "Samuel took one look at Eliab and thought, "Surely this is the Lord's anointed (I Samuel 16:6, NLT)!" But, it wasn't until he went through all the brothers except for the last son David that it became evident that David was chosen of God and would be the next king. I am so glad that God doesn't "see as we see." God states emphatically in his word that "My thoughts are nothing like your thoughts, says the Lord. And my ways are far beyond anything you could imagine (Isaiah 55: 8, NLT)."

I am very thankful for that! Why? Because many of us would have been neglected and over looked if God's selection of his people were based on the outer self. But as we see clearly highlighted in scripture that God is not so much concerned about a person's outward appearance but what is on the inside. For example, in scripture when the Pharisees tried to make it (appear) as if they were deeply religious God rebuked them with this statement "For you are like whitewashed tombs-beautiful on the outside but filled on the inside with dead people's bones and all sorts of impurity (Matthew 23:27, NLT)." In other words, any person can wear the mask and act as if they have it "all together" but God knows the true motives of a person's heart and these men had no depth nor substance inwardly and was unclean and contaminated in the eyes of God.

Furthermore, Jesus addresses this in the Book of Revelation "I know all the things you do, that you are neither hot nor cold. I wish that you were one or the other! But since you are like lukewarm water, neither hot nor cold, I will spit you out of my mouth (Revelation 3:15, 16, NLT)!" God wants our obedience and surrender to his will and purpose for our lives not our dead works. He doesn't want us consuming our time trying to make our outward selves look good and inwardly we are a mess. Our lives must be a true and holy representation of the Lord otherwise, "If we are salt that has lost its flavor, then we are useless and will be thrown out and trampled underfoot as worthless (Matthew 5: 13, NLT)."

I know we as people put a lot of effort into making ourselves look good physically and correlate that to who we are as people but we are so much more than the way we look. Even when choosing mates women and men have their idea of the way their mates should look but the "Bible tells us not to be overly "concerned about the outward beauty of fancy hairstyles, expensive jewelry, or beautiful clothes. But, that we should clothes ourselves instead with the beauty that comes from within, the unfading beauty of a gentle and quiet spirit, which is precious to the Lord (I Peter 3:3, 4, NLT)."

And, the Bible also tells us that "the human heart is the most deceitful of all things and desperately wicked (Jeremiah 17:9, NLT)." I have seen many good looking men and women but they were very arrogant, prideful and mean-spirited towards people. So, focusing on the outer man leads us all down a path of disappointment and destruction when we make it our focus as opposed to the inner man and making sure we are being made into the image of God and operating according to his purpose and plan for our lives because in actuality, that is the true epitome of beauty and wholeness, a life surrendered and obedient to God! I desire for God to work on my inner self that I will be more like him and serve him faithfully and it is my prayer that God will transform you inwardly as well to "be holy as he is holy" (Leviticus 19:2, NLT) and live life faithfully for him as well.

When we look at the Inner Man Verses the Outer Man, there are many characteristics that needs to be highlighted for learning:

Outer Man:

- Extreme concern with the things of the world. Worldly Focus. (I John 3:15, 16, NLT), (Galatians 5:19-21, NLT)

- Fleshly Motivated (I Peter 4:3, NLT)

- In Enmity and Rebellion against God (Romans 8:7, Ephesians 2:15, 16, James 4:4, I Samuel 15:23, Proverbs 17:11, Hebrews 3:8 and Jude 11)

- Influenced by Satan (II Corinthians 11:3, Genesis 3:13, II Corinthians 11:13-15, Acts 5:3)

- Leading a Destructive lifestyle (Romans 6:23) (I Peter 4:3, NLT)

- Recompense: Hell and Damnation (Luke 13:24-28, Proverbs 27:20, Matthew 5:22, 18:9)

- Inner Man:

- God Focused (Leviticus 19:2)

- Holy and Righteous Lifestyle ((Galatians 5:22-25)

- Close Relationship and Connection with God (Romans 12:12, Acts 6:4, Ephesian 6:11)

- Influenced by the Holy Spirit (Ephesians 5:8)

- Leading a Productive Lifestyle (Galatians 5:22) (I Thessalonians 4:1-11)

- Reward: Eternity with God (John 3:16, I Thessalonians 3:16-17, NLT)

As you look at the different functions of the Inner Man Verses the Outer Man, you fall into either category. Although that may be the case, my prayer is that if you are currently on the side of the (Outer Man), that you will pray and seek the Lord to save you and transform your life and enable you through the work of the Holy Spirit to disassociate from the Outer Man ("old man") and operate according to the Inner Man ("new man"). Don't be fooled by Satan and people because things are not always what they appear! Let your focus and motivation for what you do in life and who you desire to be, be in alignment with the will of God for your life.

The outer man perishes day by day and no one is promised eternity on earth. Everyone has their "appointed time to die and then the judgment (Hebrews 9:27, NLT)." Don't wait too late to make "your election and calling sure (II Peter 1:10, NKJV)." Jesus loves you and desires for you "not to perish but have eternal life found only through him (II Peter 3:9, NLT)." Even now as I am concluding this article, God is waiting for you to come to him but the decision is ultimately yours. Don't reject God but give your life to him because he has suffered, bled and died for your benefit. I am glad for my relationship with God and although I am imperfect and a continual work in progress, God is perfect, my refuge, my strength and my shield and I wouldn't exchange my relationship with him for anything that this world has to offer for he is unequivocally number one above all things in my life!

For You to Ponder: God is more concerned about our internal transformation than our outer transformation.

The Lost and Found

"Rejoice with me because I have found my lost sheep (Luke 15: 6, NLT)."

NOT THAT LONG AGO, I was packing to leave for a brief and "much needed" vacation. I am very structured and well organized and have a very meticulous system of where everything is placed and needs to be i.e. clothes, accessories, jewelry, and passports. My home front functions in like manner and it would appear that nothing seems to "bypass my peripheral vision." I function at my optimal performance when things are harmonious and in its proper order. That is why it came as an overwhelming shock to me when I arose from my bed several months ago to get ready for this particular trip and I seemed to have misplaced my peridot birthstone ring.

This ring holds a tremendous "sentimental value" in that, it was given to me over twenty-five or more years ago by my mother. I remember it distinctively. I as a child, would go by this local jewelry store and oftentimes beheld this beautiful peridot birthstone ring in the stores display window. I really wanted the ring and when I went home, I told my mother about it and that I would desire to have it as a birthday present. My mother informed me at the time that she couldn't afford the ring but would purchase something else. I was greatly disappointed and would continuously walk past the store hoping and praying to get the ring as a present.

Time elapsed, about a full year, I thought for sure the ring was no longer available but to my surprise, on my thirteenth or fourteen birthday, my mother took me by that same jewelry store, expressed to the jeweler her desire to purchase the peridot birthstone ring. I was so elated and overjoyed and thanked my mother for her extreme sacrifice and unwavering love towards me. I held that ring so dear to me. I often cleaned it along the way. I rarely took it off my finger and repeatedly expressed my thanks to my mother. As I got older and would go and visit my mother, she would oftentimes look for the ring and see it on my finger and then make the response, "You really cherish that ring don't you and have maintained it well."

That is why when I seemed to have misplaced my ring, my finger seemed "lifeless" without it. I remember finally going to my mother later on and articulating to her my great disappointment at losing my ring. She responded that, "It's Ok, and hopefully you will come across it at a later date!" That didn't suffice nor relieve my frustration. I repetitiously searched around my house to look for my ring to no avail! This fueled my frustration and I said to myself, "Will I ever find my ring or is it a lost cause?" So, finally I ceased in my efforts to find my ring and I went on my vacation and enjoyed myself despite the great loss.

Later on, I was asked again by my mother, "Did you ever find the ring?" My response sadly was "No!" Time continued to pass and finally, the "wonderful and unforgettable day transpired!" I was going about my usual day "as normal" and came home after a long and tedious workday. I was so tired and wanted to do nothing other than take a long and luxurious bath to relax mind and body. So I started the water in the bath tub. I went to get my "bubble bath" to put into the water and then used my hands to manually distribute the bubbles around the tub. As I proceeded to do this, I noticed something was trapped in the "water drainage" area of the bathtub and overwhelmingly and too my extreme pleasure it was my ring! "Well look at that!" My ring, All along it was sitting in the water drainage area of the tub. Luckily, my tub has a plastic strip inside the drainage area and that kept it from going down the drain.

I am so thankful that after much searching, tears and frustration that what was "lost is now found" and I leave these few words of inspiration. "Never give up! Keep on searching whatever "that" maybe. I was searching for my ring, what are you searching for? Whatever it is at the appointed time it will "manifest itself" (Luke 15:8, 9, NKJV)." Don't be discouraged at the time that have elapsed, don't be discouraged at the obstacles that you may encounter or don't even be discouraged at the level of frustration that you may feel because feelings aren't reliable. Just keep moving forward and don't stop until you acquire what you been looking for because it is a beautiful feeling to come out victorious on the other side!"

For You to Ponder: If you search for God, you will find him and he will bring meaning and satisfaction to your life. Prayer: God, my God, I need thee, at every moment, at every second, I am lost without you. Come into my life and bring balance and peace to my troubled mind, body and soul, in Jesus name.

The Marks of a Great Woman

IN THE WORLD THAT we live in we are constantly inundated with so many different images of women. We are told by the media, friends, family and our mates what "they" perceive a woman should be. Everything is considered from her weight, height, career, the makeup and clothes she wears from the people she is associated with. But as we delve deeper and really understand ourselves and who we are, we are faced with a "truth" that is hidden amidst all the rhetoric. The "truth" is that we are valuable, significant and carry a greater responsibility as women that far surpass our outer extremities. As we look at wonderful images of women all around us we must ask ourselves, "What are the marks of a great woman?" "Surely, it isn't in her lips, hips and fingertips?" The marks of a great woman can be categorized as such:

- Dependable-a woman who is great is one who can be depended upon no matter what (Proverbs 31:11, 12, 15, 21, 27, NKJV)! She is accessible when needed and she can be a great sense of encouragement to others even though she herself has her own struggles.

- Hard Working-A woman of greatness is good with her hands (Proverbs 31:13, 16, 17, 24, NKJV). She can create opportunities for herself through her inventive spirit. She is creative, resourceful and always committed to going beyond what is required to produce the most effective results. When people tell her she can't, she tells herself, "Yes I can!"

- Helpful and Generous-A woman marked by greatness is one who not only has trailblazing spirit and is prosperous in all she does, but one who has a generous spirit towards others and is willing to share all the knowledge, wisdom and resources she's garnered to help other women succeed as well (Proverbs 15: 19, 20, NKJV).

- Teachable-A woman of greatness is one who not only is willing to plant seeds of wisdom and knowledge into others' lives but one who welcomes insight, nourishment and wisdom imparted from other great women (Esther 2:15) and (Ruth 3:5, NKJV).

- Loving- "A great woman gives and receive love from others without limitations. She sees the best in all people. "FLAWS AND ALL!" For she realizes that all of us are imperfect people and we need to exemplify love towards each other (Esther 4:4), (Ruth 4:15) and (Genesis 24:18-20, NKJV).

- Wise- "Wisdom is Her Head Covering" She walks in it, eats it, digests it and allows it to work fully in all areas of her life (Proverbs 31:26, NKJV).

- Humble-Regardless of what condition she finds herself in life and what accomplishment she has acquired, she realizes the importance of staying humble. Realizing that with a "gentle and quiet spirit" (I Peter 3:4, NIV), you can go a long way in life but with pride and arrogance, what awaits her along the way is "a great fall" (Proverbs 29:23, NKJV).

- Modestly Dressed-A woman who is marked by greatness loves God and loves herself, and seeks to represent herself in a way that is appropriate and pleasing to God (Proverbs 7:10, NKJV).

- Trustworthy/Honest-A woman of greatness is one who makes it her aim to speak the truth. She isn't trying to be deceptive or misleading and her purpose isn't to purposely cause anyone to fall because of her actions (Proverbs 7:21-23 and Proverbs 31:11-16, NKJV). She is a sister that you can come to and know that she is going to tell you the truth, even "openly rebuke you" if necessary, with love and a desire to see you mature and go forward.

- Gentle Spirit-A woman marked by greatness is one who is gentle in her conduct. She is not loud, boisterous, aggressive or intimidating (Proverbs 9:13, NIV). She recognizes that to be a woman marked by greatness she must exemplify "spiritual inner beauty" which is an "unfading beauty of a gentle and quiet spirit, which is of great worth in God's sight (I Peter 3:4, NIV)." "Wives, likewise, be submissive to your husbands, that even if some don't obey the word, they, without a word, may be won by the conduct of their wives, when they observe your chaste conduct accompanied by fear (I Peter 3:1-2 NKJV,)."

- Takes Care of Family-A woman marked by greatness always make sure that her family is well taken care of and have all of their needs met (Proverbs 31:13-15, 21, 27, NKJV).

- When we look at all of the characteristics or attributes of a great woman I would not do just homage if I didn't mention some powerful biblical examples of great Godly women.

- Ruth: is noted as hardworking (Ruth 2:7, 17), teachable (Ruth 3:5), loving (Ruth 4:15) and faithful (Ruth 1:16-17, NKJV).

- Esther: is noted as brave (Esther 4:11, 5:1-2), wise (Esther 4:15, 5:3-8), teachable (Esther 2:15) and loveable (Esther 4:4, NKJV).

- Sarah: is noted as having "inner beauty" (I Peter 3:4-5), loyal (I Peter 3:1, 5) and trusted God (Hebrew 11:11, NKJV).

- Mary: surrendered to the will of God (Luke 1:38), obedient to God (Luke 2:1-5), (Matthew 1:24-25) and humble (Luke 1:38, NKJV).

- Rebekah: kind (Genesis 24:18-20), hardworking (Genesis 24:20) and a woman of prayer (Genesis 25:21, NKJV).

- Priscilla: is noted as being "biblically knowledgeable, humble, wise, an excellent teacher and having a good and respectful relationship with her husband.' (Roman 16:3, 2 Timothy 4:19 and Acts 18 and 26 chapters and I Corinthians 16:19, NKJV).

These are just a few exemplary examples of great women in the bible. I have been very encouraged by my research of these great women and my charge to all of us as women marked by greatness is to always make it our aim in all that we do to serve and honor God. God is at the forefront of all that we do and we must seek him and acknowledge him in everything (Matthew 6:33, NKJV). Without God we can do nothing! If we follow God's direction and walk according to his purpose and plan for our lives, then and only then can we "be women marked by greatness!"

For You to Ponder: Women are powerful, strong, courageous and gifted, celebrate yourselves, love yourselves and love who God created you to be. Look at yourself in the mirror and say to yourself: "I am _name here_,

I am loved and valuable to God and I have been created for God's divine purpose.

What Has Caused Your Leprosy?

Scriptural Reference II Kings 7:3-11

THANK THE LORD FOR his indescribable gift of the Holy Spirit and him bestowing upon me the Spiritual Gift(s) that I have to be utilized for his glory! I pray that this sermon article will ministry to every reader, someone is set free from every entanglement and bondage of Satan and consequently surrenders their lives to the Lord which is the best decision that they will ever make in their lives.

As we take a look at the word Leprosy extracted from Wikipedia, the free encyclopedia, "leprosy also known as Hansen's disease (HD), is a chronic skin infection caused by the bacteria Mycobacterium leprae[2] and Mycobacterium lepromatosis. The disease takes its name from the Latin word lepra, which means "scaly" and while the term "Hansen's disease" is named after the physician Gerhard Armauer Hansen. Leprosy is spread between people. It is believed to occur through a cough or contact with fluid from the nose of an infected person. Leprosy occurs more commonly among those living in poverty and is believed to be transmitted by respiratory droplets. Social stigma has been associated with leprosy for much of history, which continues to be a barrier to self-reporting and early treatment."

I thought it necessary to define leprosy so that every reader can clearly understand what it is and to help me clearly pontificate my message to every reader. As duly noted earlier in history, if someone had leprosy they were considered an outcast and shunned by everyone around them. It was hard for them to seek help, food or any care because people were afraid that being in close proximity to them would increase their probability of getting infected. This causes me to be deeply contemplative about many homeless people. Although I have never heard of any homeless person having leprosy, people have a tendency to treat them as such. Nowhere can you go and not see homeless people around you, for as Jesus so eloquently expresses in the Bible that "you will always have the poor among you (Matthew 26:11, NLT)." So, it is so sad when I observe how homeless people are shunned, mistreated, belittled and even mocked for the simple fact that they are homeless which similarly I am pretty sure that is how leprous people must feel because of their condition.

As we take a look at scripture specifically in II Kings chapter 7, we are introduced to four leprous men. Although it isn't clear how they contracted leprosy, it was evident the effect this condition had on their social standing and dealings with people in general. As we look at the first few verses, they were in a dilemma, they were hungry and they had a skin condition that was contagious but despite all of their problems, they knew that they couldn't remain in the state that they were in i.e. "Why should we sit here waiting to die?" We will starve if we stay here, but with the famine in the city, we will starve if we go back there. So we might as well go out and surrender to the Armean army. If they let us live, so much the better. But if they kill us, we would have died anyway (II Kings 7:3, 4, NLT)." Even though these men were leprous because of their "leap of faith," Jesus provided supernaturally on their behalf.

Furthermore, as we look at these four leprous men in the Bible, my question that I pose to you today is what has caused your leprosy? What has caused you to be considered an outcast in the eyes of people? What has caused you to be hindered in your life in some way? What has caused you to believe that just because you have made mistakes, like all of us have that, that "leprosy" or issue has caused you to cease from moving forward? What has caused you to feel as if you have no hope because life as marked you as "contagious' or "unclean." Whatever the case may be, Jesus knows where you are and he is in the business of bringing wholeness and meaning to your life i.e. "Suddenly a man with leprosy approached Jesus and knelt before him. "Lord," the man said, "If you are willing, you can heal me and make me clean." Jesus reached out and touched him. "I am willing, he said, "Be healed." And instantly the leprosy disappeared (Matthew 8:2, 3, NLT)."

Isn't it very refreshing to know that you have a Heavenly Father that loves you? You don't have to feel that you are alone and that you are struggling with "leprosy" whatever that is representative of! Many Christians or people in general have decided to disassociate themselves from many religious organizations today because of the mistakes that they made along the way and they have been made to feel like they were a leper. Instead of people coming to them and embracing them with the love of God because "God is love" (John 3:16, NLT), they were met with legalistic, authoritative, dogmatic and power posturing behavior from other Christians or "people of God." They were also made to feel that because of their mistakes, they would have to remain in the "condition that they were in!"

But, "what is the case with man isn't the case with God! God doesn't just throw us away because of the mistakes that we have made i.e. the example in the Bible of the "prodigal son" (Luke 15:11-24, NKJV). "Even though the young man left home and spent his inheritance on wild living and found himself broke and homeless, when he "came to his senses" and returned home, he was met not with scorning nor with contempt but, with love and acceptance. Not only was that, but a feast and celebration prepared for him." What a powerful example of God's love and openness to embrace us as human beings. He understands that we are imperfect people and that we "come from the dust (Genesis 2:7, Ecclesiastes 3:20, NLT)." That is why he sent Jesus to be the atonement for our sins (John 3:16, NLT). And, that is why we don't have to look to people but look to "God which is the author and finisher of our faith (Hebrews 12:2, NKJV)."

To add and for our learning, let us take a look in the Bible at another powerful illustration of God's unconditional love and forgiveness towards his people. In the Bible, we are familiar with the story of David and Bathsheba. We understand from our reading that David "set eyes" upon Bathsheba that was the wife of Uriah. He pursued Bathsheba and eventually slept with her. As a result, she became pregnant and he tried to "cover his tracks" by getting Uriah to sleep with his wife and when he was unsuccessful, He arranged to have Uriah killed (II Samuel chapter 11). David was clearly an adulterer and a murderer. David had "unclean hands" and was infected by his sins. And, the "wages of his sin" (Romans 6:23, NLT) was the loss of his son. Although that was the case, the Lord was merciful i.e. when David confessed his sin to Nathan, he replied, "The Lord has forgiven you, and you won't die for your sin (II Samuel 12:13, NLT)." I am so thankful for God's grace ad mercy towards David as well as all of us because if he wasn't we would all be destroyed.

Another example of God's love and mercy towards us "leprous people" was the story in the Bible of the "Woman Caught in Adultery" (John chapter 8). As referenced in the word of God, teachers of religious law and

Pharisees questioned God about what to do with the woman to try and entrap him. They kept demanding a response and Jesus finally replies, "All right, but let the one who has never sinned throw the first stone!" When the accusers heard this, they slipped away one by one, beginning with the oldest, until only Jesus was left in the middle of the crowd with the woman. Then Jesus stood up again and said to the woman. Where are your accusers? Didn't even one of them condemn you? No, Lord, she said. And Jesus said, "Neither do I. Go and sin no more."

Wow, what an awesome God that we serve! So, it doesn't matter what mistakes you have made because Jesus never gives up on you. People may make you feel like a leper and tell you their beliefs and opinions but what is going to matter in the long run is that God has the last say so! But never underestimate the effects of sin because "sin is a disease" and is very contagious very much like leprosy.

In conclusion, hear the totality of it all! God loves you. God cares about your current condition. God is not like man "For his thoughts are nothing like our thoughts and his ways are far beyond anything we can imagine (Isaiah 55:8, NLT)." Your life is not over and God is not through with you yet! You may have had "leprosy" and have been told that you are "unclean" but you are the perfect specimen for God to work through and bring about spiritual transformation and healing in your life. And, to use your life, your "sin disease" or mistakes you have made to enable you to be an effective representative for his kingdom and therefore be a tremendous blessing and encouragement to others.

For You to Ponder: Don't allow your past, people or circumstances to place a mark on you as "unclean." God loves you in all of your messiness and if you surrender your life to him, he will use all that you have gone through to give you a powerful testimony, spiritually transform your life and thus allow you to impact the world for his glory.

While It Is Yet Time

"No man has power over the wind to contain it; so no one has power over the day of his death. (Ecclesiastes 8:8, NLT)."

ALTHOUGH GOD CREATED MANKIND and "breathed life into his nostrils" (Genesis 2:7, NIV), it wasn't his original intent for mankind to die. As we see exemplified in scripture, it was Adam's disobedience to the directive of the Lord, that caused death to come into fruition i.e. "But of the tree of the knowledge of good and evil, thou shalt not eat of it: for in the day that thou eatest thereof thou shalt surely die Gen 2:17." As we have always been reminded of even from the beginning of the earth, there are always dire consequences for disobeying God and isn't anything that any of us should take likely. Knowing that death is very much a part of our lives, it behooves us to make it our aim "to make our calling and election sure" (II Peter 1:10, NKJV). "We Have No Time to Waist."

While it is yet time, we should strive to make sure we are living our lives to the fullest and the way in which we do so is in relationship with God. If you feel the Lord is "pulling at your heartstrings" and is trying to draw you closer to himself, don't resist him but surrender your whole life to him in obedience for the Bible states "But all who reject me and my message will be judged on the day of judgment by the truth I have spoken (John 12:48, NIV)." Surrendering your life to the Lord and allowing him to orchestrate your life is the best decision you can ever make for as the word of God states Jesus came that we all could have "life and that more abundantly found only through him" (John 10:10, NIV) for Jesus is the "way, the truth and the life (John 14:6. NIV)."

While it is yet time, we have to look beyond ourselves and look for ways in which we can bless others and empower them in different aspects of their lives, particularly, sharing the Gospel of Jesus Christ to others, so that, they have an opportunity to experience "true life" found only through Christ. For we can go through life acquiring wealth, building a name for ourselves and trying to gain prominence and be in the spotlight to prove a point to ourselves or try and please others. But, who benefits as a result of that, No one but self!

And the Bible states expressively "what profit is it to man to gain the whole world and loose his soul (Mark 8:36. NIV)." It is better to live a life of significance and one that is founded on being "other's focus" than "self-focused." When I die, I know unequivocally "without a shadow of doubt" that I don't want it to be said that I lived for myself and never did anything to bless others around me and to create change in the world for the better.

While it is yet time, let serving the Lord and obeying him be your top priority in life, as well as, how you can better serve and outwardly express love towards others. "Yet you do not know what your life will be like tomorrow. You are just a vapor that appears for a little while and then vanishes away (James 4:14, NASB)."

For You to Ponder: What do you what to be remembered for? Is it fame, is it fortune, and is it for the many accolades that you have garnered? What? I implore you to wake up every day and live your life on purpose. A purpose that is God focused and others focused and not self-focused. Begin by asking the Lord, "what would you have for me to do and who will you direct me to, to bless and encourage today?" If all you have done in life is acquired things, you are not living life to the fullest. Life living is: "Thou shall Love the Lord thou God with all thy heart, and with all thou soul, and with all thy strength, and with all thy mind; and thy neighbor as thy self (Luke 10, 27 NKJV)."

"You Are Not Alone"

"I will never leave you nor forsake you (Hebrews 13:5, NKJV)."

I LOVE THE OPPORTUNITY to walk alone at times for I find that it is very therapeutic and allows me time to meditate and spend time with God without distraction. But, sadly, there are many people in the world that are alone not because they want to be but because of tragedy, lost and broken relationships. For example, an elderly couple that had been married for sixty years and then all of a sudden, the husband dies and leaves his wife behind and then shortly thereafter you hear of her dying as well!

This reaffirmed to me how relational we are as human beings and how we have been created on this earth to be a part of each other lives. We are not an "island unto ourselves" and we need relationships in order to adequately function. That is why, in the beginning of creation, God created the woman for the man for he stated "that is wasn't good for man to be alone (Genesis 2:18, NLT). "As we look at our health and the benefits of relationships, statistically it has been shown that a happily married couple lives much longer than a single person. We need people in our lives for it is hard to go through challenges and difficulties on your own. But it is a great source of strength and encouragement to have someone in your corner that is "your cheerleader" and supports you along the way!

But what if we don't have those great support systems and people in our lives? Well, you are definitely not alone. God is the greatest father, friend, confidant and support system anyone can ever have. Even though we need people in our lives sometimes people aren't there when we need them to be, even the best of us, but, irrespective of that, there is one who will stick closer to you than anyone and that is God! For "God is our refuge, a very present help in the times of trouble (Psalms 46:1, NKJV)." For the word of God expressively states "Give all your worries and cares to God, for he cares for you (I Peter 5:7, NLT)" and God also promises us that "When we go through deep waters, He would be there for us. When we go through rivers of difficulty, we would not drown, as well as, when we walk through the fire of oppression, we wouldn't be burned up, for He is the Lord, our God, the Holy One of Israel, Our Savior (Isaiah 43:2, 3)." Now who do you know can make such promises and then keep them? No one, only God. That is why it is so reassuring to know who your true source is! I know who my source is and that is why I seek the Lord for his help daily and his will to be performed in my life for his glory.

Don't ever allow circumstances, people that walk out of your life or anything that may transpire in your life to make you think you are alone for God is always near and open to your cries and is never too busy to hear you when you pray and commune with him. He is without a shadow of doubt our "Abba Father" (Romans 8:15, NLT). God loves you very much and not a day goes by that he isn't watching over your life and keeping you safe from dangers unimaginable. In conclusion, when you are tempted to start feeling overwhelmed and feeling like you are by yourself and that no one understands your pain and all that you are going through, affix your eyes on God! Remember that Jesus came on this earth, suffered, bled and died for your benefit. And, he doesn't make that supreme sacrifice for a person that has no value. He considered you so valuable that he atoned for your sins and for mine and that atonement, within itself, is a true testament of his unconditional love for all of mankind!

For God so loved the world so much that he gave his one and only Son, so that everyone who believes in him will not perish but have eternal life (John 3:16, NLT).

For You to Ponder: Divorce, Financial Struggle, Job Loss, Family Dysfunction, whatever category you may fall under, you are not in it by yourself. God is omnipresent and God has promised to "never leave you nor forsake you (Hebrews 13:5, NKJV)." God loves all of mankind and there isn't nothing that God can't do, for God can do what no one else can do and when he makes you a promise that he is going to bless you, it doesn't matter the circumstances because he always keeps his word (Hebrews 6:13-14, NLT).

You Shall Have What You Say

"The tongue can bring death or life; those who love to talk will reap the consequences (Proverbs 18:21, NLT)."

HAVE YOU EVER HEARD it enunciated that you have to be careful what you ask for? Why? Because words are formidable and because you shall have what say. In the Bible Jesus emphatically states that "It's not what goes into your mouth that defiles you; you are defiled by the words that come out of your mouth (Matthew 15:11, NLT)." For example, you can be a person that is very indomitable and industrious but if you are incessantly negative and self-sabotaging with your words, you can thwart yourself from moving forward and living your best life.

The word of God uses a very powerful illustration of the tongue i.e. "No one can tame the tongue, it is restless and evil, full of deadly poison. Sometimes it praises our Lord and Father, and sometimes it curses those who have been made in the image of God (James 3:8, NLT)." If used properly, the tongue can be very beneficial and helpful to others and ourselves as well but, if used improperly, it can separate even the "best of us." That is why marriages, ministries and people's overall relationships with each other have been terminated and have caused irreversible damage because someone within that relationship decided to utilize words the wrong way. Don't ever underestimate the impact of you what you verbalize for the Bible states in (Mark 11:23, NKJV) "If you speak to this mountain and don't' doubt but believeth those things that you say shall come to past, then you shall have what it is that you say."

As I further ponder the significance of words and the fact that you shall have what you say, I know inarguably, I would much rather use my tongue and the words that I utter as a means to bless and empower people, than to belittle, degrade and/or tear them down. I would also rather speak words out of my mouth that will prophecy blessings over my life than say something that will curse my future. I don't care how my circumstances may look or how I may feel, I recognize the importance of saying the right things. Now, that isn't to say that I have always done that, but at this phase in my life, I choose to speak life!

In the Bible in Genesis chapter one, when God created the earth, he said "Let there be . . . " and it was manifested according to the words that he spoke. Why? Because God is infinite, powerful and the orchestrator of all things and He knows the power of words and the impact that it has in the lives of all people. Contrastingly, The Bible also declares that "We must all be quick to listen and slow to speak (James 1:19, NLT)." I believe that in choosing to be "slow to speak," we are contemplative about what we should say and how he should say it and consequently, we don't just utter anything that is in our hearts for in the word of God it specifies that "The wise don't engage in empty chatter. What good are such words (Job 15:3, NLT)?" A person that utilizes Godly wisdom is very prayerful and selective with the words that they use for "A word fitly spoken is like apples of gold in settings of silver (Proverbs 25:11, NKJV)."

Have you ever seen a person that has an "untamable tongue" and just says everything that comes to mind? If you have, you have come into the presence of what the Bible describes as a foolish person. Why? Because they are without self-control and that is a dangerous position to be in and so many people can be hurt in the process. I know that the "laws of the land" indicates that we have freedom of speech. But with that "freedom of speech" comes a great responsibility and that isn't to use the laws established to abuse and degrade others but to be very mindful of what you say that will in the long run exhort and bless others.

In summation, I implore you again, don't use your mouth or tongue loosely! Be careful of the words that proceeds out of your mouth. Why? Because wars, divorce, death, family disunity and destruction can be avoided if we think before we speak! If you have a problem in this area, ask the Lord to help you as David did in (Psalms 141:3, NKJV) to "Set a guard over my mouth, Lord; keep watch over the door of my lips." And, instead of allowing the hardships and struggles that you are encountering in life to cause you to speak "death" to your situation, try speaking what the word of God says that "I can do all things through Christ that strengthens me (Philippians 4:13, NKJV)." "I shall live and not die and declare the works of the Lord" (Psalms 118:17, NKJV) and "Greater is he that is with me, than he that is in the world (I John 4:4, NKJV)." In doing this, you are speaking life over yourself and you shall ultimately have what it is that you say!

For You to Ponder: Speak Life.

Your Body Is Precious to the Lord

It is true, yet it is sad to say, but we live in an overly sexualized society. Everything that you view on television and various other forms of media are concentrated on sex. Why? Because sex sells. From clothes, jewelry, cars, food and any other products, sex is the underlying theme. It is no wonder why people have such a very misguided view of sex and oftentimes use it in such shameful and unnatural ways.

Although that may be the case, we as people don't have to be "brained washed" or coerced into that mindset or way of thinking. We have to realize that in the beginning God created sex for both man and woman within the confines of marriage and to "be fruitful and multiply" (Genesis 1:28, NKJV). He didn't intend for us to use our bodies as a dumping ground or as a means to just sexually gratify our flesh. More often than not, I hear stories of people who are mocked and ridiculed because they choose to abstain from sex until marriage. People make them feel as if they are "out of touch," and are "not in keeping with the times." There is a lot of pressure on people to "just do it" and no one seems to be articulating the fact that sex outside of marriage is wrong and that there are many spiritual as well as emotional consequences to their actions.

Yes, consequences. Because you "reap what you sow." Or as the word of God clearly exemplifies, "Can a man take fire to his bosom, and his clothes not be burned (Proverbs 6:27, NJKV)." Sin is a "forest fire" and its effects can be devastating. So, don't ever let anyone minimize the effects of having sex outside of marriage because there are many consequences of not doing things God's way. Your body is precious to the Lord and it is to be used for his glory. "Or do you not know that your body is the temple of the Holy Spirit who is in you, whom you have from God, and you are not your own (I Corinthians 6:19, NKJV)." When we choose to commit sin in any form, we step outside of the protective covering of God and are on a downward path of heartache, pain and destruction.

Your body is precious to the Lord. Love God and love yourself enough to take care of the body that he has given you and not use it to gratify your flesh. For the Bible tells us to "flee sexual immorality. For every sin that a man does is outside the body, but he who commits sexual immorality sins against his own body (I Corinthians 6:18, NKJV)." God can't dwell within an unclean temple! So make sure your temple is clean from impure thoughts, unforgiveness, hatred, and other sins that will keep you separated from God and make it your aim every day to:

1. "Present your bodies a living sacrifice, holy, acceptable to God, which is your reasonable service and do not be conformed to this world but be transformed by the renewing of your mind, that you may prove what is that good and acceptable and perfect will of God (Romans 12:1, NKJV)."

2. "Be Holy, for I the Lord your God am Holy (Leviticus 19:2, NKJV)."

3. Again, "Flee sexual immorality," For you were brought at a price; therefore glorify God in your body and in your spirit, which are God's (I Corinthians 6:20, NKJV)."

4. And, "Let us hear the whole conclusion of the matter: Fear God and keep his commandments, for this is man's all. For God will bring every work into judgment, including every secret thing, whether good or evil (Ecclesiastes 12:: 13-14, NKJV)."

And finally, remember that you are a jewel that is precious and to be cherished. There is no one like you for you are "fearfully and wonderfully made by the powerful hands of God (Psalm 139:14, NKJV)." Recognize your value and worth and that your body is precious to the Lord!

For You to Ponder: You are precious in the eyes of the Lord. Recognize your value and know that you have been created for a greater purpose in life.

Submitting to God's Divine Will and Purpose for Our Lives

"Trust in the Lord with all your heart, and lean not on your own understanding; in all your ways acknowledge Him, and He shall direct your paths (Proverbs 3:5)."

As I SIT AND inhale the various aromas and fragrances of God's creation and is enamored by the wonderful scenery all around me, I begin to think to myself about God's goodness and his unfathomable love that he consistently exemplifies towards all of mankind. The Bible tells us emphatically that God so loved the world that he gave his only begotten son that whosoever believeth in Him would not perish but have eternal life (John 3:16). I don't know of anyone that cares about all of us that much that they are willing to sacrifice so much for our benefit. We as human beings always passionately expresses our deep longing and desire to be in a committed relationship with someone that loves us unconditionally and when we don't receive that "agape" type of love we feel incomplete. Well, there is no need to look in any other direction when looking for love because the world's viewpoint of love is contaminated by deception, greed and pride, but God is the epitome of what love is!

Although it is clear that God loves us all of us as people and his arms are open to all who surrender themselves to him, there are steps that we as human beings need to take in order for us to be in a divinely orchestrated relationship with our heavenly father. First and foremost is to fear God and submit to his purpose for your life. The Bible tells us the "the fear of the Lord is the beginning of wisdom (Proverbs 9:10)." You are wise to allow God to be the orchestrator of all areas of your life. You must recognize that he alone is sovereign and knows the paths that we should take from beginning to end, once you realize this and relinquish your desire to be in control of your life, you are now headed in the right direction.

Not only should you fear God but you should also be fully surrendered to him. The ways in which you do this is to "take up your cross and follow him daily and is to be "kingdom focused" (Matthew 10:38) (Matthew 6:33) (Proverbs 11:30), now too many that may seem to be an "impossible feat" but if you truly want a relationship with God, you are willing to make the sacrifice. The Bible tells us to trust in the Lord with all our hearts and lean not to our own understanding, in all our ways acknowledge him and he will direct our paths (Proverbs 3:5)."

Obedience and Love are also vitally important when purposing a closer walk with God. In fact, they are indispensable! In the Bible Jesus clearly verbalizes that "If you love Me, keep My commandments (John 14:15)," and "to obey is better than sacrifice (I Samuel 15:22)." We can say repeatedly that it is or desire to have relationship with God and serve him, but, if we don't do what he asks us to do, we are not in true connection with the father. "Our obedience to God is a clear indication of our love for the father."

Additionally, Repentance and Confession are key components in establishing a closer walk with God. Actually, in order for us to have a good relationship with the father, we need to "make what is wrong in our lives right." We can't continue to live in sin and glorify our "flesh" and say that we want to make our paths "straight" with the Lord. For in God's word he clear articulates, "You shall be holy, for the Lord your God am holy (Leviticus 19:2)." That means living an exemplary life that pleases God in all we say and do! There must also be an acknowledgement of our sinfulness (Psalm 32:5). You must recognize that you are the "walking dead" and in need of Jesus to revive your dark and sinful soul. Jesus, in his word gives a clear directive, "Repent for the kingdom of heaven is at hand (Matthew 3:2)." God is soon to come and it is imperative that we align ourselves with his will and purpose for our lives. Don't wait thinking that you have time because "time waits on no man." When God returns make sure you are ready!"

Furthermore, trusting God is another way to highlight our connection with the Father. In order for us to love someone there must be a certain level of trust. Trust and love are interchangeable. When we trust someone fully there is a great level of intimacy and we share with that person things we will never share with anyone. We literally trust that person with our lives. If we are going to trust anyone the most dependable person is God for the Bible clearly tells us to "trust in the Lord (Psalm 37:3)."

And also, "humble yourselves under the mighty hand of God, that he may exalt you in due time (I Peter 5:6)." God don't like prideful people. Anything that we do, we do it out of our love for God and to help others and not to glorify ourselves. When we adopt this mentality in the overall process God is glorified and that is the way that it should be! And, please don't forget that once you've confessed and repented of your sins, ask the Lord into your heart. For the Bible states "ask, and it will be given to you; seek and you will find; knock, and it will be open to you (Luke 11:9)."

Finally, the way that we grow in closer relationship with God and in Godly wisdom as a whole is to ask God for it. For the Bible states, "if any of you lack wisdom, let him ask of God, who gives to all liberally and without reproach, and it will be given to him (James 1:5)." God is open and ready to transform our lives and guide us in the best direction of our lives. He is all powerful and we as Christians or people in general must consult with him in all areas of our lives.

For You to Ponder: Trust God and let him orchestrate every arena of your life!

Practicing Lip Service Instead of Life Service

"God will judge everyone according to what they have done (Romans 2:6, NLT)."

MANY PEOPLE GET MARRIED every day and there are no shortage of ceremonies that transpire at different times during the year. People incorporate a lot of time, energy and money to make sure the wedding festivities are perfect and a day that the couple will never forget. When the day actually comes, the "soon to be bride and groom" are very excited and anxious and prepares themselves accordingly. Finally, they are marching down the aisle and are professing their love for one another and vowing to commit to each other for life.

But I wonder, amidst all of the excitement of the day, were the couple deeply contemplative of all that is required of a married couple or to make a marriage work? When they vow to "love and cherish each other, to be there for each other through sickness and health, for richer or poorer or until death do we part," do they really understand "the words that are proceeding from their mouths" and that they will encounter tests and storms in life that will test their devotion and commitment to each other, if it is really genuine and heartfelt, or, if what they have professed before God and each other was "just practicing lip service instead of life service?" Because like it or not, many couples that "have gone before them" "have been there and done that." They were excited, ready to get married and really anticipated having a successful and blessed marriage but, along the way, the "tie that bound them" didn't sustain them and when "testing" came, the "cord was easily broken."

This makes me think about our relationship with God. Many of us when we first became Christians and began our journey with the Lord, we, as many couples, were excited and willing to go the "extra mile" in our dedication and service to the Lord but, as time passed and trials came, we seemed to waiver and the same vows we made to the Lord to love, to obey and to service him faithfully, was replaced with "practicing lip service instead of life service." But God requires more from us. Our relationship with God is daily growth and renewal and it should never be taken likely. God has endured so much for our benefit (John 3:16, NKJV) and we should show our constant appreciation by taking up our cross and following him daily.

Also, in the Bible, God lets us know expressively that if "we love him, then we will keep his commandments (John 14:15, NLT)." Love is action and if we love God, then it will be exemplified in our daily lives and our dedication and commitment to the Lord. We can say that we love the Lord "a million times" but if that isn't illustrated in the life that we live then again, we are just practicing lip service instead of life service.

And, remember that "taking up your cross" requires extreme sacrifice because it isn't about you but it is all about God. I remember in my spare time watching a segment of the Steve Harvey show and Devon Franklin and his wife Meaghan Good were guests on the show. In the segment, they talked openly and expressively about celibacy. Devon Franklin talked about as a result of taking a vow of celibacy with Meaghan while they were dating and refraining from sexual active for a full year and until marriage, it blessed him spiritually, emotionally, relationally and in his life in its totality. I was so blessed to hear a man talking so passionately about sexual purity and desiring to do things God's way. And, as he sacrificed his own desires to please God, bless himself and bless Meaghan, which would later become his wife, so we can make the extreme sacrifice to obey and faithfully fulfill God's divine purpose and plan for our lives.

I don't know about anyone else but I pray to the Lord for help daily through the work of the Holy Spirit that he will enable me to be a faithful and obedience servant for his glory! Because as the Bible states that "God will judge everyone according to what they have done (Romans 2:6, NLT)." In the conclusion of the matter, we don't have time to waste! There are innumerable opportunities to be "light shinners" in a dark and wicked world. Someone needs God in their life and is the walking dead. Don't keep talking about what you are going to do in the kingdom of God but pray and seek God for his direction and that his will be done and then do what he says! And, I pray that all of us will not let our lives be about lip service but about life service and dedication to will of God for our lives.

For You to Ponder: Let your life be utilized as an instrument for the Lord, to bless others and to draw them closer to God!

Trust God

"Trust in the Lord with all your heart and lean not to your own understanding; In all your ways acknowledge him and he will direct your paths (Proverbs 3:5, NKJV)."

WHAT DOES TRUST LOOK like? Webster's Dictionary define trust as "confidence or faith in a person or thing." When we truly trust someone, we allow that person access to our lives, our "intimate space" and our vulnerabilities. We tell them secrets or other information we regard as confidential because we place our confidence in that person, even at the risk of being disappointed because there is no one that we can fully trust other than God. People change, situations change, relationships change but God never changes.

The word of God expressively tells us "not to trust in a friend or not to put our confidence in a companion (Micah 7:5)," "He who trusts in his own heart is a fool (Proverbs 28:26)."

Nothing is scarier than trusting others or ourselves more than God because he is consistent and we are not. Many of us in life have had a family member, a spouse, a friend or otherwise tell us that they would always be a source of strength or help when needed, and oftentimes more than not, when we really needed them, they were not assessable. Why? Because we can't expect something from people they can't give. We are all flawed individuals with many issues and it is hard for anyone to be fully present or available to anyone else, when they are deeply saturated with struggles and issues in their own lives.

That is why it is imperative to trust God in all things for God is "our refuge a very present help in the time of trouble (Psalms 46:1)." I know that it may be difficult for you to trust anyone because many of you trusted people that were not so kind and didn't have your best interest at heart. But, God isn't like man. He has promised in his word that "he would never leave you nor forsake you (Hebrews 13:5)" and we can take him at his word, for the Bible states that "God is not a man that he should lie, nor a son of man, that he should repent (Numbers 23:19)."

So, when life seems to be unbearable and you have people or "forces" around you telling you to give up and "throw in the towel," remember to trust God. Because the race isn't given to the shift nor the strong but he that endures to the end (Ecclesiastes 9:11) (Matthew 23:13)." God loves you very much, he sees all that you are going through and those that trust God are never alone but have a friend that is closer than any brother and cares for you!

For You to Ponder: There is peace unfathomable for those one who places their trust in the Lord!

"What Do You See?" I see a Jasper Stone a Woman of Great Value and Precious to God

"She is more precious than rubies (proverbs 31:10, NLT)."

HAVE YOU EVER ASKED yourself this question? Never mind what people may say because they are always trying to compartmentalize you and fit you into their own idea of who they believe that you are. When I look at myself in the mirror I love what I see, "flaws and all." I tell myself what the word of God says that "I am fearfully and wonderfully made" (Psalm 139:14), that God has a wonderful plan and future for my life (Jeremiah 29:11), that "I am blessed coming in and blessed going out" (Deuteronomy 28:6), that my worth is far above rubies" (Proverbs 31:10), that "I am the head and not the tail, above only and not beneath, a lender and not a borrower (Deuteronomy 28: 12, 13)."

We as women of God and people in general, must recognize our significance and that we have been "made in the image and similitude of God" (Genesis 1:27), (James 3:9). God sees us as precious and a very necessary part of creation and that is why in the beginning God created woman from man. God did this because man was alone and he indicated that it wasn't good for man to be alone (Genesis 2:18).

As you look around you what do you see? I see many great "jasper stones" that have contributed innumerably to our society and the world as a whole! Women are strong and powerful in so many ways that is why God chose us to be the "givers of life." Don't ever let anyone belittle you or devalue your noteworthy contributions to life. It takes extra motivation and drive to be a woman. Women have to be "multitaskers" within the home, "multitaskers" at work and "multitaskers" in life.

There is no one set thing that a woman does, we contribute in varying ways from being mothers, wives, nurses, leaders and the "list goes on and on." And with juggling many tasks simultaneously, we still manage to "look good" and keep the family intact! All of these things are noteworthy and that is why we as women everyday should encourage each other because no one "can do it quite like us." We are a precious jasper stone in the eyes of God and valuable to life. God put us on this earth for a reason and that isn't to be a "doormat" for someone to walk over, not to act as a harlot or a dumping ground for every man, not to walk behind a man but beside him and to be good leaders, mothers, sisters, friends, colleagues and in all that we do on this earth will help and impact people's lives for the better and thus give glory to God!

For You to Ponder: Your value and worth is not of this world because it is found in God.

"Hold on to Your Dreams and Don't Let Go"

TIME IS FLEETING AND tomorrow isn't promised to no one. We don't have time to waist. We must realize the value of life and that it is a gift from God and that we have been placed on this earth to impact others and to bring glory to God. Although that is the case, we must also not devalue our gifts and talents and allow the daily struggles, failures or difficulties to hinder us from pursuing our dreams and moving forward with our lives.

I have seen over the years countless people that have given up on their dreams because with every attempt to progress and accomplish their goals, they have faced many obstacles, barriers and blockages. "No one ever said that anything worth having would be easy." Life is a series of struggles and "quitters never win." It takes tenacity, perseverance and an unshakeable resolve to keep getting up after you have been knocked down several times.

Life is like a boxing match:

The two components prepare themselves physically, mentally and emotionally before entering into the ring. They go into the boxing ring with one mindset and that is that there will be "one winner and one loser" and thus, they go in with the expectation they will be the winner. That is how we as people need to be with life and with meeting our goals and aspirations. You can't be so easy to "throw in the towel" because the fight is intense and you sustain a few harsh blows along the way. That is not the time to give up, but that is the time to muster up the strength, position yourself in faith and fight until you come out on the winning side.

Below are a list of other things that are needed to hold on to your dreams and don't let go:

1. Don't allow people, lack of resources, negative talk, or otherwise to deter your vision.

2. Ask God for help, guidance and direction in your life.

3. Stand on the promises of God, you can trust him when you can't trust no one else.

4. Hold on and don't let go until God blesses you.

For You to Ponder: Live life to the fullest, take life by the wings and soar!

Acknowledgements

I JUST WANT TO give honor and glory to God for this opportunity to be utilized as an instrument for his glory for I realize that there is nothing that I can do of myself, for he has blessed me with every spiritual gift to be utilized for the advancement of his kingdom and that his will is performed on "earth as it is in heaven!" Everything that has been written in this book is practical, informative, thought-provoking and encouraging to all who read it. We as people need to understand that despite our many struggles and difficulties in life that we are not alone for God is present, God is able and God can rectify our issues.

I had to learn this in my own life and I am still learning this lesson every day in many different phases of my life. And, it isn't until we come to the end of ourselves, trust God and fully surrender to his will for our lives that we experience true peace and are able to see God's powerful hand move in miraculous ways in different facets of our lives. So, in the finality of it all, I love you all in Jesus name and it is my pray that whatever you need God will provide, but mostly importantly, you will surrender your life to Jesus and let Him be your Savior and your Lord!

Thank God for all that I've suffered in life because in the process of it all, God birthed out the idea for this book and blessed me in many ways to be a blessing to many people that I can sympathize and empathize with their struggles in life. I am very appreciative to Jack and Jaarr my two "best guys" and support systems through it all, they know of the struggles and thank God for their patience with me through this process, I love you both very much and, thank you profusely to the publishers and for them giving me "the green light" to move this project forward. If they hadn't take a chance on me and allow the Holy Spirit to lead them in the decisions that they made, this book wouldn't have been published. I pray many blessings and continual success to you all and in all of your endeavors in Jesus name.